Make Your Career Meaningful: A Practical Toolbox

James Patterson

Copyright © 2015 James Patterson

All rights reserved.

ISBN: 1507712719
ISBN-13: 978-1507712719

DISCLAIMER

The opinions expressed in this book are my own ideas, based upon my personal experiences as a recruiter for more than 23 years. My intent is to stimulate proactive activities for taking charge of a career path, not to replace any licensed career or psychological counseling.

CONTENTS

Acknowledgements

1	The Impact of Work and How it Affects Us	1
2	What We Offer to Our Employer	11
3	Knowing When to Change Jobs	29
4	How to Determine the Right Job for Us	43
5	Interviewing Tools and Preparation	58
6	Weighing the Pros and Cons of a Job Offer	81
7	Why Did We Not Get the Job	87
8	We Got the Job, Now What?	97
9	Better Ways to Manage Our Anger, Fear and Guilt	108
10	Changing Dysfunctional Workplace Beliefs	129
11	Using Gratitude and Forgiveness to Improve Our Relationships	145
12	Building Patience and Tolerance	165
13	Finding Meaning in Our Work	179

James Patterson

ACKNOWLEDGEMENTS

My heartfelt gratitude goes out to my wife Mary Lou for her many years of support and understanding. She has given me her kindness, wisdom, and love.

I am also grateful to my family, friends and colleagues for their encouragement and support.

Special thanks to a physician friend who opened my eyes to the influence our minds and emotions have on our workplace environment. His insights served as the motivation behind many of the ideas in this book.

Chapter 1: The Impact of Work and How it Affects Us

Work has a massive impact on our lives, simply due to the amount of time spent on the job. If we have a full career, this is equivalent to 10.7 years of working 24 hours per day.

This book contains my common-sense, practical experiences with more than 200,000 clients and candidates encompassing a wide range of ages, areas of expertise, seniority, as well as different temperaments and personalities. The forthcoming chapters will stimulate new ideas and approaches to self-evaluation, job selection, interviewing, and building character. The challenge of career development never ends but the reward is new responsibilities along with refining our knowledge, values and expertise.

The idea of "work" or "career" can suggest an

idealistic situation where we see ourselves surrounded by caring and thoughtful people. Our work environment can be creative, challenging and respectful as we look forward to each new day and the opportunities it brings. Perhaps our work nourishes us and we are appreciative and thankful for all it offers. We might feel valued for our efforts and inspired by helping others.

Instead, we might associate work with despair as we march off to the office every day. We can feel helpless, as we have no other legal way to earn a living. We might be dismayed about the drudgery of a mindless job and cringe as we approach the beginning of our workweek. We can feel powerless because we have an obnoxious boss who gives us little respect, words of kindness or encouragement. Our high ambitions might have come to naught, as our opportunity for advancement never materializes. We may feel unappreciated, abused and disrespected.

On the other hand, perhaps we see work as somewhere in the middle of these two examples; we have taught ourselves to accept the work environment with its vicissitudes. It is *just a job* and some days are better than others, so we find ways to adjust and get by. We recognize we need to work to support ourselves and do our best as we develop enjoyable work relationships. Our thoughts and discussions frequently turn towards retirement, vacations, holidays, personal interests or buying that new house or car we always wanted.

Work influences our lives in many ways:

- Our work environment includes the culture of our company, the working style of our managers, and how we relate to them. Do we enjoy or simply tolerate our work environment? We also have coworker relationships that can inspire or distract us each day.
- Our job function—does it interest us? Do we think our job is important? Do we feel valued for what we do? If we find our work boring and our efforts lacking in value, we may begin to see ourself as unimportant and unworthy.
- Work creates various opportunities for growth through promotions, learning new skills, or serving others.
- We can find meaning in our work by overcoming difficulties and incorporating our values into our daily tasks.
- Because our work consumes so much time, we may reorganize our free time more efficiently by learning to prioritize with more effectiveness, determine what is most important and stop obsessing about the small stuff.

- We receive a paycheck that enables us to handle our financial obligations and pay for outside interests.

Work affects our home life as we manage the invigorating and stimulating parts of our job versus our work failures or regrets. While bringing home our successes can uplift our entire family, our disappointment, anger or bitterness can trail cloudiness and despair wherever we go. *Big trouble can occur when we bring home stress or irritation that occurs at work.* Building a wall between work life and home life is not a positive solution; however, we can learn the difficult skill of compartmentalizing our activities by shifting our general outlook from what is appropriate for work versus what is suitable to our non-work situations.

Our work can result in frustrations and anger. If unresolved, our anger takes residence in our subconscious and:

- adds to our general discontent and disappointment
- negatively impacts our physical and mental health
- damages our relationships
- contaminates our attitudes about everyone we come into contact with

- is the expression we wear no matter how hard we try to hide it.

We know stuffing away our negative emotions or responses is not the answer. In order to manage anger or frustration, we need to develop skills and knowledge for our mental and emotional selves. *In effect, we need to "shower" off the psychological dirt and grime that comes from a difficult day at the office.* This requires self-control and new skills that I will discuss further in later chapters.

We create and execute plans each day, be they plans for birthday or wedding parties, vacation trips, going out to dinner, or even what program we will watch tonight on TV. However, in the case of our career, our plan will require a more complex set of skills, including many we may not have yet developed. Our career will not magically prosper on its own. We cannot expect ourselves to have a meaningful, exciting and productive career unless we create it ourselves.

Knowing the impact work has on our life, it behooves us to create and execute a plan for career development that:

- places us in the right work environment that meets our needs for growth and relationships.

- builds the strong mental and emotional components of our character that help us overcome difficulties, achieve goals, handle setbacks and interact with others.

The purpose of this book is to serve as a roadmap to creating a meaningful and successful career. It is not all-encompassing, but it does describe a variety of subjects including:

- understanding our expertise and knowledge
- clarifying our career decisions and path
- reflecting on why we should make a job change
- knowing what constitutes a good job fit for us
- various interviewing tools
- common interviewing mistakes
- how to integrate into a new company
- the importance of building new skills
- building character
- finding meaning in our work
- managing ourselves through the trials and tribulations of the workplace

I have found it personally distressing to witness people struggling with their careers. For many, this starts as they graduate from high school or college.

They may have mastered the ability to excel in academics but their knowledge is frequently not applicable to success in the workplace. There is little training available in schools to land a job based upon a good fit between employer and candidate or the tools necessary for long-term success. In addition, there is a lack of training in self-evaluation or recognizing what they can offer other than enthusiasm and a willingness to learn. If they are fortunate, they might have guidance from a mentor, but this is not common.

Thus I frequently see recent graduates make two to three quick job changes as they attempt to move beyond their innate talents. This growth in understanding often means learning what it takes to be successful, what is a good work fit for them and how to manage their mental and emotional responses to the demands of the workplace. For example, they may have to learn a sense of urgency, attention to detail, communication and organizational skills, interpersonal and analytical skills, and how to effectively manage workplace conflicts.

On the other hand, I also observe many people who are in their mid-careers and have established a pattern of success in the career process. *While there are exceptions, most people tend to continue with what has worked in the past and there is little attention given to more personal analysis of who they are, how they interact with others, what their career goals are, and what else they can do to improve their situation.* Thus, they miss future opportunities and stay within a narrow range of experiences and options. The tragedy in this is that they do not continue to grow or pursue new expertise and understanding. *Over time, their sword of knowledge and skills will dull due to repeat use and lack of sharpening.* I have experienced thousands of examples of this group of people becoming less useful to their employers and ultimately fired. This often comes as a rude awakening and, unfortunately, it is all too common. The solution for all mid-career people is to continue aggressively pursuing new abilities, technical expertise and improving their skills in interacting with others, especially in complex situations.

Finally, I have worked with people late in their careers who either are trying to finish out their last few years in the workforce or are struggling to understand why their career has been less than fulfilling. They are unable to translate their many years of experience into a meaningful sense of deep satisfaction that comes from realizing their significant contributions over a lifetime. *This is a disaster because as we come to the end of a career, we should be on the top of our game, not just trying to get by.* Our years of experience should translate into wisdom and sophistication, as we know who we are, where we can best contribute, how to handle difficult people, and how to deal with our own regrets in a healthy way. Unfortunately, if we have failed to continue to learn and develop, we can become outdated and our many years of small or large disappointments can eventually weigh on us. We feel burned-out and out of date, and find ourselves crammed with the toxic accumulation of years of cynicism, apathy and dejection. This does not need to happen.

Do the above issues or deficiencies exist with all of the people I have interviewed? No, of course not. Some people have carefully worked on their career by constantly reinventing and updating themselves. They have learned from their mistakes, know how to handle loss and integrate their core values into their daily activities. This requires a working plan and effort.

Planning a career path does not guarantee that there will not be problems along the way. However, the act of careful planning and reflection gives us a much better chance to achieve our goals and end a career with a deeper sense of meaning and satisfaction. This book will delve into the logistics of how to do so. This is our opportunity and we can seize it!

Chapter 2: What We Offer to Our Employer

A successful business recognizes the need to have a competitive product or service. This starts in the conception phase of product development as the features and benefits are laid out and it is determined how they apply to a given market. The product is then built and refined around these parameters and specifications.

In the same way, this is how to create a viable and productive contributor to a given organization. It all starts with planning the key features and benefits we can create within ourselves and then building the necessary skills, knowledge and character for our future employer.

As part of this process, we must start by understanding what *raw* material we have to work with. In other words: "What are our skills and knowledge, how do we relate to others, how do we manage our difficulties and what are our values?" While this type of analysis might appear to be a simple process, for most people it is not. I frequently ask people in an interview to tell me about themselves. The most common answers I receive are: "I build good relationships"; "I know my job"; and "I have a strong work ethic." While these are valid answers, they lack depth and barely touch the totality of who they are as people and what they can offer to a company.

In addition, some employees' opinion of their own contributions to their company is inconsistent with what others observe. Sometimes they overestimate their contributions—and, surprisingly, sometimes they underestimate their contributions. They may also see themselves as kind and thoughtful, yet others see them as overbearing and selfish. *Virtually everyone claims to "work hard" but working hard does not necessarily translate into working productively or effectively.*

So why is there such a disconnect between how some people see themselves versus how others observe them? *My observations are that many people find self-evaluation difficult because they have not given it much prior consideration. Self-evaluation brings them face-to-face with their low self-esteem, disappointments, regrets, laziness or possible self-absorption.* Working through dysfunctional parts of our personalities or observing our mistakes and shortcomings can be painful. We would rather not explore this part of ourselves, or perhaps we do not know how to do so. Simply put, admitting our weaknesses can be quite difficult.

People also do poorly at self-analysis because they have built up a strong sense of themselves as competent (or not). They only look at themselves through their own specially colored glasses and see themselves as a projection of their self-image, which may not be true. In addition, *they* have a near-phobia for criticism and push it away. If self-criticism ever comes up, it is rejected immediately and considered out-of-order. They fail to recognize that self-examination can help them recognize the terrible risks of having blind spots. For example, unless we become aware of our tendency to be overbearing or contemptuous, we can sabotage relationships and turn off people.

Sometimes people are hypnotized by familiarity as they blandly assume that whatever they do (attitudes, beliefs, intention, motives, action plans) is okay because this is what they have always thought and done. It never occurs to them, for example, that being angry about insults or feeling discouraged about partial failures is not a healthy way to respond. *They assume what they always do is the only and correct way to do things. This is the "tyranny" of the usual and familiar.* Thus, most people do their best to get by and fail to realize the huge growth opportunity available to everyone who practices self-examination. I will write on some of these issues later in this book.

So how do we go about this process of self-analysis? We can start by breaking down our analysis into several sections. These sections include our aptitude related to specific business skills for a given type of job or role; our personal character that includes our relationship skills; and, finally, our values. These are critical components of who we are as an employee.

Business-orientated skills

The following is a list of business-orientated skills. This is not an exhaustive list but contains many of the skills requested by clients I have worked with. We can look at each of these skills (or add our own), determine our level of competency and then work on them as needed.

- **Technical**: specific knowledge or expertise about a given role.

- **Commercial awareness** (or business acumen): knowledge about how a business or industry works and is successful.
- **Organizational**: general organizing, planning, prioritizing, time management, scheduling, coordinating resources and meeting deadlines.
- **Problem solving**: using analytical and solution orientated ideas to solve problems and create new options.
- **Communication**: a combination of verbal, written, and listening skills.
- **Negotiation**: a dialogue between parties intended to reach an understanding, resolve points of difference and craft outcomes to satisfy various interests.
- **Team Player**: work performed by a group of people, with each doing a part but all subordinating personal prominence to the efficiency of the whole.
- **Leadership**: ability to motivate others, assign and delegate tasks, set deadlines and lead by example.

We must honestly access and have a realistic view of how skilled we are in these areas; we gain nothing by assuming we are better or worse then we actually are. We need to understand that we all have emotional or mental "body guards" that we use to protect ourselves from self-criticism and possible emotional pain. These "body guards" get in the way of self-evaluations. We need to disarm them in order to give ourselves honest feedback. *Also, self-evaluation does not mean berating ourselves and belittling our faults and mistakes. We use this information to improve ourselves.* If needed, we can also consult with other mentors or friends for input, to assure us we are realistic in our self-evaluation.

People who are high-achievers understand the importance of business skills and are constantly looking for ways to improve themselves. There is never a time when they think they have learned everything there is to know about a given skill. Instead, they have a plan to improve their skills, "sharpen their swords", and work on them each day. With consistent effort, we too can improve our skills to make us more marketable as job candidates and better valued as employees.

Personal Character

We need to look beyond our business skills and evaluate our personal character. In my experience, this area receives less attention than it deserves. Even talented employees often place their emphasis on getting the job done, achieving the numbers, or accomplishing their goals.

They might also feel they can do little when it comes to their personal character because "they are who they are" and this is unchangeable. They do not always recognize that how we achieve our goals and the way we are perceived and work with others is critically important. I have watched people *blow up* an organization or *their team* when accomplishing their goal. While they may enjoy the satisfaction of achievement, the price they pay in terms of damaged relationships, hurt and angry feelings, and loss of trust and respect are significantly detrimental to their long-term success.

Surprisingly, personal character is the main component of each individual that is most often remembered by their associates. When I talk with the references people provide for job applications, these references have *some* knowledge of the business skills of their associates and can grade their level of achievement. However, the part they readily remember and generally have the most admiration (or distaste) for is the person's character. *Character is the glue that can hold together relationships, build respect and loyalty, create affection and a strong sense of connectedness—or destroy all of these things.* I have noticed that as people approach retirement, they speak with affection about the various important people they have known over the decades and it is the character of these individuals that stands out.

The following is a partial list of exceptional qualities of character that hiring companies find admirable. One might argue that some of these are also business skills, and they are, but they are more than that. These qualities transcend the workplace and they are the values we hold and the way we behave and relate to others in all personal interactions, not just at work. These qualities can also be enhanced; we are not limited to the qualities of character we have developed at this point. Instead, we can build on these qualities and incorporate new ones. I will write in later chapters how this is done and use several character qualities as examples.

- **Personal Responsibility/Self-Control**: taking full responsibility for our achievements and disappointments, including our emotional and mental responses to events. We own the results of how we respond to life and what we have achieved.
- **Integrity**: adhering to high standards of various work processes as well as personal and professional conduct.

- **Respect/Honoring and Valuing Others**: recognizing and respecting different perspectives, open to the ideas and views of others, and viewing the contributions and uniqueness of others as significant.
- **Patience**: understanding that growth and development of projects and people require time and effort; the state of steadfastness or endurance under difficult circumstances without becoming excessively annoyed or upset.
- **Perseverance/Drive**: determination to achieve a goal and constantly looking for better ways to do so. Work presents many difficulties and perseverance enables us to continue our efforts, even when challenged.
- **Self-Awareness**: awareness of our achievements, abilities, values, weaknesses, temperament, strengths, and life purpose.
- **Trust:** firm belief in reliability or truthfulness as it relates to someone or something.
- **Self-Improvement**: regular and committed improvement of one's mind, emotions, character and overall business skills through individual effort on a regular basis.

- **Flexibility**: physical, emotional and mental adaptability to changing situations and environments
- **Creativity**: the ability to create meaningful new ideas, forms, methods or interpretations beyond the traditional ideas, rules, patterns, or relationships; continually believing there is more to learn and better options to consider.
- **Forgiveness, Gratitude, Patience and Tolerance**: these will be written about in detail in a later chapter.

Anger, Fear, and Guilt

I will write about the qualities of anger, fear, and guilt in more detail in a later chapter. However, I want to note that our emotional responses to events are part of who we are, how we relate in the work environment, and are a serious component of our ability to succeed in various roles. I have seen many examples of talented people with great skills and even good qualities of character run aground when they are unable to manage their emotions during difficult times in the workplace. We are not meant to be held captive by our own emotional and mental outbursts; instead, we can take charge of how we respond. This enhances not only our workplace environment but our personal life as well.

LPV Analysis

There is one other type of analysis that I have found useful. I refer to this as a LPV Analysis and it stands for Like, Proficiency, and Values. I use this tool with various candidates to give them perspective about who they are and what is likely to be a good fit for them in various jobs in the future. Here is how the exercise is used.

The candidate writes down over a period of a few days or weeks all of their daily activities at work. They should eventually have two-hundred or more activities on this list: for example, making phone calls, talking with various managers and associates, writing reports, attending meetings, solving problems, building or creating products or services, conversing with friends at lunch, and working on the computer. Also, an activity should be counted as separate if it involves a different focus. For example, we can be on the computer to order things, do research, enter data or write. This would be an example of four activities on our list.

Once we have our large, detailed list (the more activities, the better) we are ready to perform the LPV analysis on these activities. We first look at each item on our list and ask the question, "Do we like this activity, or not?" We do not ponder it at length. We answer with a quick "Like" or "Do Not Like"—similar to what people do on Facebook. There is no neutral response; "Like" or "Do Not Like" are the only options. Through this exercise, we determine which of these activities we prefer or enjoy.

The next step in the process is to run through the same list again and ask ourselves the question, "Is this activity in an area where I am proficient?" Once again, the results are either "Yes, I am proficient" or "No, I am not"; there is no middle ground. We must also be honest with ourselves; as we answer this question, self-deceit is not useful. If we are uncertain, we can ask a trusted colleague about our proficiency in a given area.

Having asked and answered these two questions about all of these activities, we now have a grid of four possible responses to each activity. For example, we might find that we like computer research work and think we are reasonably proficient at it. In another example, we might find that we do not like dealing with an irate customer on the phone but we are actually quite proficient at it. Our grid of four possible answers to each activity includes: Like, Proficient; Do Not Like, Proficient; Like, Not

Proficient; and Do Not Like, Not Proficient. By reviewing this grid, we can view our likes and dislikes versus our proficiencies for our normal activities.

There remains one final question to use on this list of activities. We ask ourselves, "Is this activity consistent or not with the values I hold most important?" There is again no middle ground for an answer; it is either consistent or not. Values are those noble principles or standards that deeply move us and create meaning in our lives. As we review our list of 200+ activities, not every activity is likely to express our values. However, we want to note those activities that express our values such as exceptional service to others, kindness, gratitude, self-control, our achievement of a challenging goal or overcoming a significant obstacle.

So what can we conclude from this type of LPV analysis? How can we use this information to tell us more about ourselves and what might be a good career fit? Here are some thoughts to consider:

- If we look at our entire activity list, we should see patterns that give us some idea of how we relate to our work. This information illustrates what types of tasks we readily like (enjoy or prefer); what areas we are proficient in; and how our values relate to these activities. For example, we might be proficient interacting with people, or perhaps we are better suited to work that involves analyzing data. We might enjoy a work environment that emphasizes creativity, or we might prefer a role that is more structured. Our values might focus on trust, respect and integrity, and thus we need to be part of a team that honors these qualities. *Ideally, we want a job where we enjoy the majority of our tasks, we are good at them and they uphold and allow us to express our values.*

- We might find we subtly detest parts of our roles we find boring, monotonous, trivial or overly detailed. We might dislike other work because we cannot stand the people we work with. These experiences can slowly poison our work experience and fill us with gloom and despair. We need to find effective ways to manage this discomfort rather than simply accepting our negative responses. I will write about this in later chapters.

- We can investigate what draws us to certain activities and, on the other hand, why we avoid other tasks. Is there a message here? Perhaps our lack of proficiency and concern about being embarrassed restricts our activities. We can manage this by refining our skills. Frequently, better training will ameliorate our anxiety about working outside our comfort zone and will give us more confidence to enjoy our activities.

- We can look deeper into ourselves as we observe our likes and dislikes. Do we always take "the easy road" and avoid issues that might bother us? Do we focus only on what makes us feel good? If so, we should better manage the part of us that strictly wants comfort, because the most challenging issues usually result in the greatest growth. Indeed, our discomfort can incentivize us to learn new skills and knowledge. Some people give up too soon and fail to learn how to overcome various adversities. Unfortunately, these issues are likely to materialize again in the future, presenting new challenges either in their current company or at a new one.

- All work or life activities include some areas that we do not enjoy, are not proficient at and that do not uphold our values. It is impossible to avoid this entirely. Therefore, we must learn to accept these situations and find ways to avoid distress.

- We want to look at how we couple our likes and proficiencies with our values. Our values will sometimes override our likes and proficiencies. This alerts us that the price we pay for working through a difficulty is valuable and meaningful, even if it is arduous. I have heard many stories over the years of people working through difficult projects with difficult people that required long hours and struggles. They frequently remarked they did not enjoy the whole process and were not always highly skilled at such tasks, but they embraced the work anyway because they valued the end goal. This created meaning and satisfaction in their lives.

Many candidates start first with their career goals, rather than beginning with a thorough understanding of themselves. I think this is a backwards approach. *We need to know ourselves first.* Have you ever seen someone's career skyrocket before failing? I certainly have. After their promotion, are they overwhelmed? Do they lose their self-control or fail to anticipate future needs? Do they let fear, anger or guilt influence the way they relate to others? *How many people do you know fail to clearly and honestly see themselves, and in turn create easily avoidable problems in their personal and professional lives?*

We need to know the following before we set our goals:

- What are our values and how do we integrate them into our work?
- What are our deficiencies and how can we correct them?
- What are our most enjoyable and proficient areas of expertise?
- What are realistic achievable career goals based upon our ambitions, talents and willingness to do the work?

You might now be thinking that all of this self-analysis is a lot of work. Well, it is! You might also think you already know yourself and there is nothing left to learn. You are wrong! What could possibly be a better goal than to understand more about who you are and what you can offer so you can grow in your career?

As I wrote about earlier in this chapter, it is not possible to improve ourselves if we do not have a clear picture of whom we are and what we want to build. This is a huge effort because, as we do the hard work of transforming ourselves, we frequently have to subordinate our personal desires for comfort or our unwillingness to admit our deficiencies. The payoff in our professional lives is that we will become better employees, more valuable to our companies, and more eligible for promotions.

Are there other ways to do this type of analysis? Can we take a test somewhere that tells us who we are, how we think, the nature of how we relate to others, and what our preferences are on many issues? The answer is there are many such tests on the market and I have heard people remark on the utility of this type of testing. *However, my main point is that whatever the source of the information on ourselves, we must actively apply it to the hard work of personal development.*

Chapter 3: Knowing When to Change Jobs

A job change can be an exciting and fulfilling experience. It can bring us:

- new opportunities to develop and express our skills, knowledge and character.
- an introduction to new people, challenges and problems to solve.
- a possible significant bump in pay or responsibility that is consistent with our career goals.

These are some of the upsides to a well-thought-out and well-executed job change.

Our process of making a career change begins with deciding it is time to move on. Frequently, the decision to leave our company starts with either: 1) discontent with our current job; or 2) the allure of a more substantial opportunity from another company. Sometimes the decision to change jobs is an easy one, for example when our misery level with our current firm is very high, or when the new opportunity is substantial. However, this is not the usual scenario.

More often, a job change is complex and elicits various emotions and conflicts within us. We may:

- feel torn between our loyalty to our current firm and the allure of a bigger job at another company.
- enjoy our current colleagues but worry about future unknown relationships.
- feel insecure and question our ability to be successful in another firm.

We can also ask ourselves if we are leaving to get away from an uncomfortable experience? It is easy to be emotionally upset as we respond to a bad day at the office, a difficult time with a manager, a setback in our career advancement, or feeling unappreciated and overworked. These events can motivate us to look for employment elsewhere—but is that the right decision?

It is possible that our boredom, dissatisfaction, or discouragement with our current employer may be our own creation. In that case, a new employer will not solve the problem. I have observed many people who were motivated to escape and moved to a new job, anticipating great results. However, they failed to realize that some of their negative issues at work were their own issues that then followed them to a new job.

As we start exploring other options, the newness and excitement of an anticipated job change can draw us in like a magnet. We fill ourselves with hopeful anticipation of good things to come. We are like sponges, soaking up new facts and information as well as the attention showered on us. However, the fluffy feel-good experience that comes from being recruited and starting a new job eventually goes away.

Thus, we need a plan for making a career change. We need to:

- evaluate our motivation for changing jobs and how we determine a good fit.
- assure ourselves a new employer can meet both our short-term and long-term needs.
- match up our skills, working environment, desire for advancement, need for challenge, and our emotional makeup.

The following are a list of common reasons or motivations to change jobs. Under the right circumstances, they are all valid, reasonable, and make sense. However, we need to look carefully at our decision process and our patterns of behavior. Are we always running away from these issues of boredom, discouragement, a poor work-life balance, a bad work environment or feeling unappreciated? If so, maybe we need to rethink our decision process. In the following sections, I write about each motivation for change and reflect on various ways of evaluating these internal motivations.

Boredom

We might feel bored with our current employment. Most people enjoy the opportunity for challenges and growth, as long as the learning curve is not overwhelming. New challenges can come in the form of promotions, new projects, or complex problems to solve. If there are not sufficient challenges in the workplace, we may become bored and sloppy, fail to grow, and eventually decide to look elsewhere.

Is boredom always a valid reason for a job change, or can we learn something else from this experience? All jobs have a certain amount of redundancy in their processes. For example, the job of a salesperson includes certain processes such as planning, probing, handling objections, closing skills, and canvassing for new clients that will always be a part of the selling method. *If we become bored with this lack of diversity in our job, we need to find new ways to create our own enthusiasm and freshness.*

As a salesperson, we might challenge ourselves to enhance our selling skills or create new ways to find or present to customers. We can do the same with other staff positions; we can learn new skills and knowledge about our work. Eventually we must find a way to get past unending boredom or our career will consist of constant job discontentment as we seek out the external stimuli of new jobs to keep us going. We become job junkies and the fix for our addiction is a new job.

We can solve our problem of boredom by using creativity to keep us fresh and inspired. We invoke creativity by continually asking questions such as:

- What can I do today to improve my skills and knowledge?
- How can I better manage this situation? Are there other approaches to consider?

- I seem to have mastered several parts of my work, but are there other areas I have yet to develop? Am I missing something?
- I have great job skills, but what about my relationships with colleagues? Can I do more to improve them or perhaps work on my own character?
- Can I work more on managing my anger or fear in the workplace?
- Do I understand my values and apply them daily in my work?

This constant habit of inquiry stimulates new creative thought that helps reduce boredom. We also need to eliminate the thought: "I have learned all there is to learn about this skill or situation." While there may be a time when we become very knowledgeable, the idea that we have "mastered" an issue for the rest of our career is a dangerous belief. There is *always* more to learn and experience.

Is boredom ever a legitimate reason to consider a job change? One can argue that a highly monotonous dead-end job that allows for no creativity would be a good reason to consider a job change, but we must balance this with other ideas. For example, is this a pattern for us? Do we find ourselves starting each new job with enthusiasm and fire in our belly, but shortly become bored again? If we quickly move from job to job, it is possible that we have chosen jobs that are not stimulating, challenging, or complex enough for our needs. Maybe we failed to investigate the best possible fit for us. Or perhaps, as I have written about above, we have failed to create our own energy of enthusiasm and newness by challenging ourselves to learn more.

Discouragement

Discouragement is difficult for some people to handle because it forces us to acknowledge our inability to achieve our goals or aspirations. For example, we might have failed to achieve a promotion, a large raise, or sufficient accolades from our managers and colleagues.

Discouragement is a call to develop and manage ourselves. Our discomfort can make it appealing to handle discouragement by running away, giving up, or using avoidance or anger. We might want to blame others for "holding us back."

We need to acknowledge that discouragement is our own reaction to disappointment; thus, it is our responsibility to fix it. Frequently the solution is to enhance our own knowledge or strengthen various talents. To assess if we are continually working to improve our capacities, we need to ask ourselves the following question:

- What have I done today to further cultivate and develop myself?

Highly productive people ask themselves this question every day. They are looking for ways to improve their game and consider learning to be a key component of that development. Even if they fail to accomplish certain goals, they do not perceive this as discouraging but rather as a new challenge. Their question in response to discouragement is: "What can I learn from today's setbacks and what new abilities and understanding do I need to accomplish this goal at a later time?"

Respected and Valued

Most people rate "respect" and "feeling valued" as critical components of job satisfaction. They want to see their work as valuable to both themselves and others and experience respect for both who they are and what they do.

While we all want others to respect and value us, we earn this in the workplace: it is not an entitlement. Do we practice respecting and valuing others? *Many people love to receive respect and admiration, but do not practice it themselves. How many sincere thoughts of appreciation do we put forth each day?* Do we understand that others participate in our own success and treat them as part of a team that supports us? Are we overly critical of others, either outwardly or in silence? This excessive criticism may be born from a need to manage our own insecurities.

Have you ever sat in a meeting and heard people complaining about sloppy work done by others? How does this compare with sitting in meetings and hearing honest accolades that speak to the great contributions people make? An imbalance of acknowledging productive and useful achievements versus berating the inadequacies of others contributes to a negative work culture. This lack of respect and recognizing value serves as an insidious cancer that eats away at the well-being of a company.

Criticism might also be a perfectionist desire to have the entire organization do things perfectly even though this is impossible. We must work to incorporate a more mature and healthy outlook about our fellow workers because an overly critical nature leads to worse relationships and increased turnover. This *does not* discount the constant need to improve deficiencies. However, there is a difference between a healthy need to offer constructive criticism versus a permanent critique that we are surrounded only by incompetent, dysfunctional people. We should strive for the former and avoid the latter.

Creating respect and value starts with us. If we want to experience it, we need to express it. It requires the firm realization that each employee is a critical piece of the working structure of the company. Using the analogy of a body, it may make sense that the senior management or *Head* of the body is the true critical part. However the *Head* is not going to get anywhere without hands, arms, legs, a good circulatory system, nervous system, etc. The entire body of the company must work in concert for a company to flourish, and we need to acknowledge this.

Just recognizing the synergistic relationships within a company is still not enough to create value and respect. There needs to be a properly developed organization, diverse companywide skills, training, leadership, clearly defined goals, objectives, and a creative vision among other things. But, respect and value starts with us and we must lead by example.

Not "Feeling Good" About Our Job

We must take a closer look at what it means to *feel good* about our job. How we *feel* is not always a valid parameter of what is best for us and how we should make decisions. For example, it might *feel good* to yell at people who upset us or *feel good* to avoid difficult situations, but is the way we *should* behave?

Some of us might *feel* unfilled in the workplace and think we need to move on. We may *feel* we need more recognition and accolades. *But, ultimately, we are the ones responsible for evaluating the quality of our work and giving ourselves suitable praise and support.* We can decide if we have done enough and whether our work is valuable. *We do not need to rely fully on the input of others.*

This does not mean that our supervisor is not entitled to analyze our work, offer advice on how to improve, or give us kudos. However, we need to carefully access this input and either accept or reject it based upon our own criteria and values. Some managers are never satisfied and others are too forthcoming with compliments that are not valid.

We need to realize that *feeling* comfortable about our work is not always the best measurement of a worthwhile job. Taking on a difficult challenge at work and accomplishing our objectives will frequently elicit the most meaningful responses. These challenges are what force us to be more patient, persevering, disciplined, adaptable, and self-controlled. This is a more beneficial outcome than just *feeling good.*

The Fit of the Daily Work Process

Regardless of our compensation or role in a company, we must enjoy the basic nature and process of what we do. It is simple: if we really do not like the details of our work, we are unlikely to excel or succeed. Leaving our job because we did not investigate the daily work process is reasonable—but it also shows our failure to access a good fit for us. This is a subject in the next chapter.

The Company is Not Going in the Right Direction

People frequently tell me a company is going in the wrong direction, but this has nothing to do with a company's stability. Instead, it is their own disappointment that their success, achievements, and work relationships are not satisfying. They may not agree with certain decisions; changes in their management; or changes in their role within the company. They have confused the phrase "right direction" as it relates to the company with their own personal wishes and desires. *We need to understand that the company's decisions might be reasonable but we just don't like them.*

Growth Opportunities

The desire to grow and advance is a common

motivation. We need to first define our goals, recognize the work required to achieve them, and decide if are willing to expend the energies and resources to do so.

Some people want to advance because there is an underlying belief that we should always be "moving up the ladder." However, we need to make sure we are the right fit for such advancement. There is no shame in remaining in a good job with great people, regular challenges, and opportunities that are consistent with our desires and developmental needs. We want to avoid leaving for a flashy job or a big promotion, and then bailing out a year or two later because we realize it is not a good fit for us.

On the other hand, there are times we have sharpened our skills and done all we can to earn a promotion. It might be that the organization cannot accommodate such a promotion because there is none available. It then becomes our decision to accept this or move on.

There are several additional common reasons people provide as their motivation to leave their company. These include *compensation/benefits, work-life balance,* and *the work environment.* We must investigate these issues *prior* to taking a job, not after we have started. They are an important part of accessing if we are a good fit for a job; I will cover this more fully in the next chapter.

Chapter 4: How to Determine the Right Job for Us

Thus far we have evaluated our character and business-related skill sets, job change criteria, work activity preferences, proficiencies, and values. The next step is identifying an ideal fit between a company and us. The following are some key areas to investigate in our quest for a good job fit.

Work Preferences, Proficiencies and Values

We need assurance that we have alignment between our new role and ourselves. Asking questions can give us information on work activities at a potential job and help us determine if they are consistent with our preferences (likes), proficiencies and values, as I wrote about in Chapter Two. We can ask these questions of our potential manager or company during the interview process:

- What is the job title? What are the key roles and responsibilities? Can I review the job description?
- What is the workflow of a typical day?
- Where can this job lead? What are the promotional opportunities?
- What are the two to three most important qualities of your best employees?
- What are the two to three biggest challenges for people in this role?
- Can you describe my working relationship with others within or outside of this department? How does their work affect my job?
- Is my job mostly self-directed or regularly supervised and structured?
- How will you measure my job performance? How can I assess if I am exceeding the expectations of the job?
- Why did you join the company? What continues to challenge you and help you grow?
- What are the key skills and knowledge required to excel in this role?
- How can you and I best work together to make my job a success?

- What can I do immediately to get off to a great start?
- How does your company differentiate yourselves from your major competitor?

We can also ask questions of ourselves as we gather more information. Some of these questions include:

- Do I enjoy and understand the technology and/or services of this company?
- Have I talked with others in a similar role and determined the subtleties and nuances of the job? Can I learn from others how management handles their employees? Can I seek out and speak with former employees to get their feedback on the company too?
- Do I have the right training and experience for the role, or can I readily learn it?
- Will this work challenge me? Can I use this role to build for the future?
- What are my "walk-away first impressions" about my future supervisor? Do I see a good match with his/her style and communication?

Work-Life Balance

People need personal time to take care of their family, manage domestic issues, and also relax and have fun. Ideally, we want our job to supply us with this type of flexibility. A balance between our work and outside activities is critical to long-term job satisfaction and helpful in reducing burnout. Here are some points to consider:

- How much time is spent on the daily commute to work? Not everyone perceives commuting as a downside, but an hour or more of daily commuting can be fatiguing, while also affecting free time. An hour each workday adds up to five hours each week, which is equal to more than one full day of commuting every month!

- What is the volume of work required for our future role? Can we put in weeks of long days, or an intense eight hours that may leave us exhausted? Do we need to work at home? Everyone has different ways to pace themselves at work and we need to match our style with the requirements of the employer.

- What are our long-term expectations with the company? Do we want a promotion, a large raise, or accolades due to superior job performance? This usually requires hard work and commitment that might include extra time on the job. The workplace is a competitive environment and companies require excellence in order to thrive. We need to recognize that putting in ten years in a company or having ten years of experience does not guarantee success. *We do not want to confuse activity with achievement.* We have to work to become more efficient and to learn new skills, both technical and interpersonal.

- What do we want out of our career? What do we want out of our personal life? It is possible that we can achieve all of our career goals while also having the external life we desire. However, if our goals include rapid career advancement and significant recognition from our company, we must be willing to put in the effort and time at work. We are not going to advance at work by wishing and hoping, but instead by developing the skills and knowledge required. At the same time, what are our goals and aspirations for our personal life? Building strong family relationships require effort, commitment and energy too.

Job Security

Due to the economy's state of flux, as well as the consolidation of various companies, job security has become more important than ever. Here are some common-sense questions we can ask to help minimize the likelihood of ending up out of work due to a company layoff, bankruptcy, reorganization or acquisition:

- Is the company growing? If the company is publicly traded, this information is readily available. Even with a privately held company, we can make an assessment based upon obvious signs of growth (such as the addition of new employees) or evaluate the company's products or services to determine if they are competitive in the marketplace.

- Look at the tenure of senior management: do they have a long-term track record of success? By reviewing press releases and research articles, we can evaluate if the overall industry is healthy and growing, or if it is experiencing mergers, acquisitions, or frequent restructurings.

- Finally, we play a large role in our own job security. *The best people in a company are the least likely to be dismissed and are the most attractive to other companies.* We need to build exceptional interpersonal and job-related skills, and find ways to add value to our company. This is our best guarantee of job security.

Opportunity for Advancement

Advancement means different things to different people. For example, people can view advancement as securing a management position, promotions, more money, or more interesting and creative projects. Some people just want to be respected for the work they do and to have a full workload each day. Some people see the quality of their work and relationships with others as a measure of success.

Having defined what advancement means for us, we must evaluate if this is possible in the short or long term. If we are interested in traditional promotions, the senior staff of the company might be long-term employees with low turnover, therefore limiting our promotional opportunities. If the company has slow growth, there is unlikely to be room for upward movement and there might be fewer creative projects. We can also investigate if a given company tends to promote heavily from within or whether they tend to look outside the company for new employees.

We must also develop our talents and earn the right for a promotion when positions become available. We must ask ourselves, "Have we planned for a promotion by developing the necessary skills and knowledge?"

Opportunity for Personal Development

Another area to consider is personal development. While traditional advancement might include more responsibilities and classic promotions, personal development involves our values. This includes the opportunity to develop our integrity, patience, thoughtfulness, creativity, humility, gratitude, perseverance and self-control. Some companies might put a premium on developing these qualities and provide formal programs to do so. However, even without a formal program, we can work on personal development and incorporate it into our daily process.

Work Environment

Creating a great work environment is partially our responsibility and we must lead by example. *In my observations, the work environment is the number-one reason people stay in or leave their jobs.* Therefore, we must carefully evaluate our work environment fit as a major component of the decision process.

The work environment includes:

- the physical space we work in.

- our daily activities.
- the support, encouragement and respect we receive from our management team and colleagues.
- the necessary training and resources to get the job done.
- new challenges to help us learn and grow.

To begin, we must establish our own standards of behavior and skills as our benchmark for interacting with others. For example:

- How do we relate to our boss and colleagues?
- Do we appreciate the support of others, or do we take this for granted?
- Do we follow-up well after meetings or tasks?
- Do we meet reasonable company goals?
- Do we show courtesy and listen?
- Do we work hard at developing new skills and knowledge?
- Are we open to new ideas? Do we attempt to see things from other perspectives?
- Do we try to be helpful and carry out our fair share of the workload?

- Are we genuinely interested in the welfare of others, as we see others as contributing to our own success?

We can also ask ourselves questions about the leadership team:

- Do we respect, admire and have confidence in them?
- Do they emulate the values of the company and treat employees and clients with respect?
- Do they adhere to qualities of character such as excellence, gratitude, and integrity, and communicate these by example throughout the organization?

Employees want respect for both who they are and what they contribute. *I find it interesting that many employees will put up with lower pay, a poorer quality product and less potential for advancement if they feel respected and valued.* A company's culture is not unlike an individual's personality. Companies can be arrogant, self-surviving, and overly demanding—or they can be supportive, creative, and grateful for their employees as the lifeblood of the company.

It is inevitable that we will encounter cranky and crabby people in all organizations. We need to deal with negativity by building skills to handle difficult people, while also retaining our optimistic and productive outlook.

Compensation and Benefits

More money or benefits do not make our job more fun, meaningful, challenging, interesting, creative or rewarding. Some people leave their jobs for money alone and become miserable because they failed to evaluate the details of the job and ended up with a poor match. We need to make sure the financials and benefits of a job are acceptable, of course, but we should focus our full attention on the details of the job, the environment, and growth opportunities that are the exciting and sustaining parts of our workday.

There must be sufficient financial remuneration to take care of our family and build wealth for the future. However, in my opinion, compensation is a logistical consideration versus a meaningful one when considering a job change. People garner meaning and fulfillment from the aspects of a job: the challenges and learning opportunities and various interactions they have with others. People do not spend all day at their desk counting their money. *Instead they are engaged in the day's activities, and this is the "payment" that nourishes them the most.*

We need to avoid worrying that a new job may not pay as much as our current job, or that some people might think it is "a step backwards." It might be a step backwards if it is exactly the same job with the same responsibilities, products and company culture—but generally, this is not the case. The important thing is that our compensation takes care of our needs. It does not matter if it mildly fluctuates up or down.

Some small companies do not have the resources to match the pay scale of the largest companies. One can then look at the decision to move to a smaller company with less pay as a tradeoff. Does a smaller company allow us to gain more responsibility, learn new and different skills, and/or use more creativity in our daily work? If we see the value in this and the compensation is still sufficient to meet our needs, this can be a worthwhile job move, not a step back.

Stock options, vacation time, and medical benefits are also part of a job offer. Once again, think of these as logistics versus the job itself. We want to make sure they are sufficient to cover our needs. If they are, we must remain focused on the details of the job in order to make the ultimate decision about whether this is a good move for us.

Other Points to Consider

There are several additional ideas or issues to contemplate as we make our job decision. They include the following:

- No company is perfect; they all contain warts and problems. During the interview process and as we are being pursued, we may become overly enthusiastic about the new potential employer and unknowingly put on blinders. *It is important to seek out any possible downsides to a new role and be realistic about our expectations.* There is no perfect company that guarantees us a stress-free job.
- A new company will not necessarily fix our problems. Our frustrations and disappointments may have their basis in our own unrealistic expectations or inability to manage relationships. We need to look carefully at our issues and take responsibility for managing them. For example, we may constantly seek out quick and easy results. We may avoid confrontation. We may crave freedom to do things our way. These issues can set us up for disappointment.
- Sometimes a friend or professional acquaintance introduces us into a company. This is valuable because we can gather inside information. However, we need to make sure this new

opportunity works best for us. I have observed people collectively jump ship to a new opportunity that adds nothing to their future. The solution to this problem is to make our own decision based upon *our own* due diligence, needs and expectations, rather than the opinion of others.

- People will frequently hear good or bad things about a company via Internet research, rumors or from friends. Listen to this input, but make an effort to gain first-hand information before making a final decision. Some of the negative comments can be based upon the bad experiences of a few angry or unrealistic people and may not represent the truth about the company.

- Some people are lured into a new job by a higher level of responsibility or a promotion. While this may seem to be a perfect situation, I have observed people accepting a role that is over their head. We must make an honest assessment of our own skills and learning abilities, and match this up with the potential job. Being overwhelmed is a recipe for disappointment.

- We need to ask ourselves if we require constant feedback, especially compliments and accolades. This can be a source of frustration for many, as they do not get the recognition they want or desire. Perhaps we need to evaluate our own insecurities and need for attention. We should work on giving ourselves appropriate feedback so we are not so reliant on others.

Chapter 5: Interviewing Tools and Preparation

Waiting to prepare for an interview until the night before, or just reviewing a few facts on your smart phone, is not a smart idea! Years ago, company information and details were hard to come by due to the lack of the Internet and the use of traditional mail. *However, today, failing to prepare for an interview is no longer an excuse and is one of the most preventable ways to not advance in the interview process.*

Acing an interview is a learned skill. Even if we think we are a brilliant interviewee, we may have never encountered an experienced professional interviewer. Our ability to impress people upfront with our *glow* and *razzmatazz* ends when a good interviewer looks beyond our first easy answers and digs further with more insightful and challenging questions.

The following are some ideas and tools to consider as we prepare to interview.

Company Research

A frequent first question from a company is, "What do you know about our company?" We need to answer this question effectively or the interview is over as soon as it started. The feedback from companies when a candidate has not done their homework sounds something like, "How can this candidate use his or her valuable time to interview here when they do not even know what they can offer to help our business?"

Prior to the interview, we should have already considered if this role is a good fit and if we are a competitive candidate. We do not need to become experts on a company, but as a minimum, we want to understand:

- their product or service
- their market
- some details about our role in the company and how we would fit their needs
- the organizational structure
- stability
- growth
- market share
- stock price

- pipeline of new products or services
- the industry as a whole, its growth opportunities and the impact of new technologies

We can also try to find a job description for our role, the potential for personal advancement, as well as information on the company culture.

Questions

Our questions are a major part of the interview process. *The questions we ask are as important as the answers we give.* Our questions can inform the interviewer:

- the homework we have done
- if we are knowledgeable about their technology and market
- if we understand our potential role and how we can add value
- our communication skills
- our business acumen

If we have not studied up on the company, we cannot ask these types of questions.

Other questions can inform us about:

- the short- and long-term needs of the company

- what skills or knowledge are required to succeed in this role
- the manager's major concerns about our candidacy
- future advancement opportunities
- the company culture
- the important personal qualities and characteristics of an ideal candidate
- the various interactions and relationships we will have in the company
- the biggest challenges for a new hire
- examples of their best employees

In addition, the interviewer's answers to our questions can help us tailor our own answers, and also inspire additional questions we want to ask about the company.

We need to customize our questions for each interviewer based upon the relationship we will have with them in the company and their current role. For example, the questions we ask a sales manager will be different then the questions we ask a research person. We should bring four-to-six broad questions for each interviewer that will generate additional follow-up questions. We can derive these questions from the bullet points above. We can also add more detailed questions that align with our likes, proficiencies and values as outlined in Chapter Four.

Questions about compensation and benefits are something that should be addressed in later interviews, not as a part of an initial discussion. However, we should have already assured ourselves that the compensation is at least in the range of what we will accept prior to considering the interview.

Our Story

We want to prepare and fine-tune our story of success and achievement prior to the interview. This story of success is not a regurgitation of our resume, but rather is a broad overview representing key highlights of our achievements, skill sets, and character. The resume already indicates the basic performance and skills of a candidate but does not define the subtleties of a person including their values, how they respond to various challenges, how they think and work with others, and what motivates them. This will come out of the interview and is a major component of why people are hired.

One way to prepare our story is to break it down into various categories as many companies do when they evaluate our fit for hire. They are looking at various performance, experience, and personality fits for their job. In my office, we use the acronym SPEARS to define these categories. SPEARS is an acronym that stands for Stability, Performance,

Education, Affect, Relevance and Sense.

We use this acronym to create a consistent and standardized approach to the interview process. This avoids the common occurrence of either a company or a candidate commenting they *like* the candidate or the company. *Like* is not a comprehensive criterion with which to make a career or hiring decision. We need to break down our interview process into more quantifiable metrics and categories.

Stability

The first category is *stability*. We use stability to evaluate the time a candidate has been with previous companies. We also evaluate the stability of their character, which reflects their ability to remain collected and focused even in challenging situations. Frequently, long tenure and mature character go together. That is, if someone is unable to maturely handle the undulations of the day-to-day process in a given job, they are likely to leave and seek employment elsewhere.

I have noted a candidate's average tenure has changed over the twenty-three years I have been recruiting. While I cannot calculate an average number, it seems that fifteen-to-twenty years ago, an average employee worked in a targeted industry with a company for five-to-seven years. In 2015, the average tenure I observe is two-to-four years. I do not know all the reasons for this change; however, my observations are this is due to a greater visibility of available jobs on the Internet and social media, leading to more job choices for candidates; less patience and a strong desire for immediate career gratification; and decreased tolerance of difficult situations in a company. The net effect of all of this is a faster turnover of people in the job market.

To evaluate stability, we talk through each person's job changes and focus on why they made each change. Their reasons are usually some variation on the theme that the company was no longer meeting their needs and it was time to move on. As I wrote about earlier, some of the specific reasons given for job change include:

- boredom
- discouragement
- lack of respect or feeling valued
- difficult relationships with bosses or colleagues
- not "feeling good" with the job
- poor work-life balance
- frustration with daily work process
- the company not going in the right direction

- poor salary or benefits
- a lack of growth opportunities and advancement

These reasons might be acceptable but I wrote about previously, a good interviewer will ask follow-up questions to determine if the candidate's motivations were indeed sound and mature.

Why people change jobs, not unlike why they change relationships, says a lot about how they make decisions and what they value. The work environment can be difficult and the key is how we handle such difficulties. Do they distract us from our tasks? Do we give up and quit? Or, instead, do we find better ways to handle adversity?

A good interviewer will look at the behavioral patterns behind why people make changes and assess their likely stability in a new opportunity. Previous patterns of job changes are usually a good indicator of what to expect in the future. Job changes are not necessarily looked upon as "unacceptable" by hiring managers, but they must be well thought-out and justified. A company will be reluctant to hire and train a person who they suspect might quit when the going gets tough or something easier comes along.

Performance

Performance represents measurable metrics related to achievements in a given company role. It might include sales numbers, product growth, quality, annual reviews, and achievement of company or management objectives. When evaluating performance, we are interested not only in the results but also in *how* the results were achieved. An interviewer may ask a question such as, "What are the three-to-four skills or qualities that most contribute to your success in each of your business roles?" Surprisingly, many candidates have not thought about this question. They might be very skilled in their job but have not taken the time to understand *why*.

Understanding why we are successful is important because it informs us of our strengths that we can build upon and enhance further. For example, is hard work or being a quick learner enough to be a top performer in a company? The answer is no. More comprehensive and insightful answers would include:

- being highly organized
- possessing great attention to detail
- persistence
- quickly identifying a customer's needs
- analytical or planning skills

- excellent communication
- creativity
- a broad approach to problem-solving

There are other skills or qualities too, but the point is we must be prepared to discuss the reasons behind our achievements.

Education

Education, of course, indicates various degrees or certificates a candidate possesses. Furthermore, it also includes what candidates do on a regular basis to further educate themselves, build greater skills and knowledge, or enhance their character. This education includes but goes far beyond company training. This might include formal class work, reading books or blogs, consulting with others, or personal and character development.

A candidate might be asked, "What have you learned recently and applied in your current job?" or "What skills or knowledge are you researching that will help your business?" We use education to indicate the ability to seek out, learn, and apply new information in work-related roles on a regular basis. The application of new insights and ideas from employees is the lifeblood of a company, and is a crucial part of an employee's ability to grow and develop. *Top performers in any job are always looking for ways to enhance their skills and knowledge.*

Affect

The fourth category *affect* refers to the energy, enthusiasm, curiosity, confidence, dynamism, creativity, presence, and communication skills of the candidate. It is how they come across and the energy they exude both on the phone and in person. One point about enthusiasm: it is more than simply being excited. It is *intelligent* energy or excitement based upon our knowledge, skills and curiosity. We exhibit enthusiasm in how we ask questions, meet our goals, and manage adversity. True confidence is not to be confused with an arrogance that says we know everything. Instead, confidence is based upon our experience, comfort and knowledge of the subject matter—while also acknowledging we always have more to learn.

Affect also encompasses our basic temperament. We are not going to change our basic temperament for an interview. A high-energy person is not going to become laid-back; a thoughtful and reflective personality is not going to become a fast talker. There are times when a certain temperament is what a company is looking for and if we do not have it, there is little we can do. However, regardless of our temperament, we can all be engaged in the interview process through good eye contact, sincere interest in the interviewer, solid preparation, and asking great questions.

Relevance

Relevance is determining if the background of the candidate matches up with the specifications of the job. Do they have the ideal type and breadth of experience or knowledge base? For example, if a client is looking for a pastry chef, our background in quantum mechanics is not applicable. Our physics background will not give our fresh-baked muffins a light and fluffy texture. Even if we argue that we have no experience but are a quick learner and will work hard, we will not likely get the job.

I have worked with many candidates who become upset when their background has little relevance and they are dismissed. This usually happens with people who have a strong sense that they can do anything— and, in fact, maybe they can. However, we need to acknowledge that the hiring company makes the final decision on who is relevant and we should not become overly discouraged if the company rejects us.

On the other hand, there are times when our background *is* closely aligned, but not perfect. For example, we might be a skilled creative cook who is versatile in the kitchen and has a good foundation in baking, but does not have specialized experience in pastries. This still would require some training on the part of the hiring company, but they are more likely to see the value of this overall experience and its application.

It is also important to realize that we may be the perfect experience match and still not get the job because in looking at the entire picture of our candidacy through a SPEARS analysis, we are not the right fit. We might have issues with stability, performance, temperament, or a lack of self-learning. The hiring manager might even have a bias against the company we worked for, the college we attended, or the color of our shoes. (Yes, I have seen candidates rejected because of shoe color.) We can do little about this.

The takeaway point with relevance is that the employer will view the candidate's entire background in the context of the employment opportunity and decide how it is relevant. Some candidates make the mistake of focusing on favorite parts of their backgrounds because they are proud of a certain experience, even if it is irrelevant to the hiring manager. *We need to remember that we are interviewing to fulfill the company's needs and focus on how our background is relevant and useful to a future employer.*

Sense

The final part of our acronym SPEARS is *sense.* When we evaluate a candidate, here we are focusing on *common sense.* Some questions a company may ask themselves when considering a candidate include:

- "Does this opportunity make *sense* from a career and personal perspective for this candidate?"
- "Is the money, title, level of responsibility and required skills a good fit for a given candidate?"
- "Would this place them in a role where they can prosper, learn, and add value to the company?"
- "Is the candidate taking a large cut in pay, does this represent a serious step down in their responsibility or possibly is it a step up that will be over their head?"
- "Does the travel and business hours work for their family?"
- "While they are smart, can they handle the learning curve in this job?"

- "Does their temperament, style and affect match up with the company culture?"

A company is looking for possible problem areas down the road. For even the best candidate, there are always some quirks and subtleties that are important to sort out. Using *common sense* helps determine if the logistics of this hire seem favorable.

As we mentally complete this SPEARS analysis on ourselves, we now have "our story." Now we can use this information during the interview to discuss our:

- history, relevance, and performance
- how we make decisions and learn
- how we can help our new company
- how we manage adversity and achieve goals
- what we value

Business Plan

In preparing for an interview, we should already have an idea about what we will do if they hire us. This is a major reason we are a strong candidate; we are bringing our previous skills and experience to a new company to enhance their organization and we will require less training and hand-holding to get up to speed.

Thus, we should come to the interview prepared to talk about our background and how it would apply to this new role. Of course, our future employer will know our role and the priority list of how we should approach our responsibilities. However, it is very common for an interviewer to probe a candidate for his or her own ideas and thoughts on how to best approach the job.

For some company roles, they may ask us to organize our thoughts on paper into either a brief business plan, a 30-60-90 day plan, or bullet points that describe the 4-6 action items we would act on first as we start the job. This information helps the employer understand how we think, organize, prioritize and execute our job functions. Some employers outline their key needs in the first interview and then, as an assignment, ask the candidate to develop a business plan as part of a follow-up interview. They are testing our ability to create a plan of action in our new job and observe how we respond strategically and tactically.

Why This Company?

We need to speak about why we are leaving or have left our previous employer and why we are interested in this specific job. We can describe how this new role will enhance our own career and, in turn, benefit our employer. We need to say more than we are *excited* about this role. We need to respond with detailed and thoughtful answers, such as describing the company's:

- rapid growth resulting in more promotional opportunities
- solid financials
- unique technology
- stable and strong management team
- mentorship and development of employees
- excellent compensation based upon performance
- leadership in their market
- stock options
- strong pipeline of new products

When asked about any previous company, we should express gratitude for our previous experiences, but our focus needs to remain on why we are interested in the new company versus talking about why we are leaving or have left our old firm. If we use the interview to complain about how bad our old companies was, we risk casting ourselves in a negative light. Even if we previously worked for a terrible company and had a lousy boss, we should not talk about it during an interview! *If there is a cardinal rule in interviewing, it is this: never complain about your previous employer.*

We should also refrain using the following reasons for our interest in a company:

- I need the money
- Good benefits
- Nice working conditions
- Easy commute from my house
- Better work-life balance
- Friendly people

While all of these reasons might be valid, they are not compelling. We have to remember that while we value such things as an easy commute, good benefits, or fun people to work with, expressing these reasons in an interview does not send the message that we are there to add value to their organization. Instead, these reasons send the message that it is all about us. We do want to satisfy our own needs but in an interview, our message is that we are there to meet our new employer's needs.

Concerns or Objections

As the interview is winding down, we should ask the interviewer for any concerns or objections. This question might be something like, "What concerns or objections do you have about my ability to do this job?" This is not the same thing as asking what the next step in the process is. We need to address any potential concerns, as the employer likely has concerns about even the perfect candidate.

A common insecurity runs through most hiring managers. It is a blend of fear from making a mistake before, wondering what they might be missing that the candidate is holding back, and worry that the candidate who looks good today might be a problem in the future. People can become moody, change their minds, forget things, give up, or become disappointed, angry, fearful, or confused. They can blame others for their problems and refuse to take responsibility. Unlike a new car or refrigerator, neither employees nor companies come with a warranty guaranteeing a reasonable time-period of good quality service.

Even the most experienced interviewers or hiring managers make hiring mistakes. Concerns or uncertainty on the part of a hiring official makes complete sense and we should be ready for it. We need to recognize that our failure to ask for concerns and then proactively address them might result in the interviewer's concerns transforming into negative impressions.

Some interviewers will ask us about our weaknesses.

We want to accompany any perceived weakness with a solution of how we are working to overcome it. For example, we might declare we take things too personally, but are learning it is not always personal. It is just the fact that people have difficult days and it is not always our fault. In another example, we might admit we can become frustrated when others are not as passionate as we are about a project, but we have learned that this is an unrealistic expectation as others are not the same as us.

We might be worried that we cannot answer all of an employer's concerns. One way to minimize this issue is to anticipate likely concerns before going into the interview. This could include gaps in our resume, a lack of relevant experience, many job hops, or a lack of performance data. We should think through the various ways we can address these issues prior to the interview and be prepared to talk about them.

There is one common concern that most people struggle with: lacking on-the-job experience. How do we handle this concern when it is the truth? I wrote about this earlier in the section on *relevance*. If our experience is completely irrelevant, we are unlikely to overcome this concern. However let's assume we have some related experiences such as the example of the cook applying for the pastry chef job. We can point out our relevant experiences to the hiring manager and clearly demonstrate how our experience applies by discussing specific examples that relate to the new position.

We can also handle the concern about our lack of experience by following up with a question of our own: "What skills do you find most important for success in this job?" In this way, we are asking the hiring manager for job skills rather than a time frame of on-the-job experience. Frequently, the answer will include a variety of qualities like persistence, great communication, integrity, quick learner, adaptable, driven and responsible. The answer could also include some technical skills. Thus, the approach to this question is to identify the skills required for the job and then give examples of how we can apply these skills without having the exact job experience.

Closing

At the end of the interview, after we have asked for concerns and objections, we want to "close" for the job. This means we thank the interviewer for their time, describe the skills and experience we can offer the interviewer and then ask to move forward to the next step in the interview process. We want to express our interest in the job even if we have some reservations.

Some people might think it is unfair to express their sincere interest in the job before they have gone home, thought about it and talked with their family. This is legitimate, but we are trying to earn the right to advance to the next step so we can gather more information and potentially receive an offer. It is important to express an interest as it shows our enthusiasm and how well we "sell" ourselves. The interviewer looks upon our interest in the job favorably and our enthusiasm is not binding; we can call back later and tell the hiring manager we have decided to stop pursuing the opportunity.

We must follow up with all the people who interviewed us via a brief email. While we can also send a handwritten note, we want to be sure to give quick feedback. In our email we want to thank every interviewer for his or her time in telling us more about the company and the position. We should mention our strong interest in the role, and what we can do for the company based upon what we learned in the interview. Finally, end the email by asking to be considered for the next step in the process. This note summarizes why we stand out as a candidate, why we are a good fit for the company and why they should hire us.

Final Comments

Interview preparation takes time and greatly increases our chances of receiving a job offer. We can help ourselves by anticipating likely questions or concerns about our own background, researching the company and its people, and understanding who we are and what we offer. A SPEARS analysis can help us with this process.

In addition, there are a few more points to remember. We should dress well, bring along extra business cards and resumes, and be engaging and focused in the interview. We can take a few notes during the interview, but be sure this does not distract from our conversation and eye contact.

Finally, I have never seen a company hire a person they really dislike. No hiring manager has ever called me up and said, "Well Jim, that candidate was a real pain in the butt along with being overly aggressive and obnoxious, but he is a great performer and we are going to hire him." *The takeaway point is that companies hire people because they are thoughtful and considerate, along with having top performance credentials.*

Chapter 6: Weighing the Pros and Cons of a Job Offer

Exhilaration and excitement come with receiving a job offer. Our homework, preparation, presentation, and handling of objections have paid off. We should feel proud of what we have achieved. However, how do we make a good long-term decision by either accepting or declining the offer?

This is an ideal time to take a step back and revisit a number of issues before making our final decision. This is likely an emotional time, and we want to feel assured that we have covered all the important points because this decision will affect us daily for months or years to come. It is a good idea to review the points in Chapter Three and Chapter Four about why we are considering a job change, what to look for in a good job fit, and to consider the following issues too:

- Have we talked over the impact this job change will have on our family? Job changes impact our family members because we will have a learning curve, will expend extra effort and attention to get off to a successful start, and our routine of travel and business hours may change. We might feel stressed out as we wrap ourselves around the new job, which could create some family tension. Is our family supportive? Is everyone ready for this transition and prepared for the changes and disruptions it might cause?

- Are we leaving our company for the right reasons? I wrote about this earlier but it is worthwhile to think through it again. Are we running away from something or are we embracing a new challenge that will help us grow and develop? If we are leaving something we do not like, are we fairly certain this new job will remove that issue? Have we considered we might be part of the problem and taken steps to correct our issues? We also need to remember that all companies have issues, even our sparkly new company.

- Are we ready to give notice and tell our old company goodbye? What will we do if they try to convince us to stay? Breaking up is hard to do and most people have a certain sense of loyalty to their old firm and colleagues. We might experience guilt or fear in leaving. This includes our gratitude to our old firm for what we have learned, the people we will miss, and our uncertainty about the future.

- We need to prepare for giving notice by writing a note tendering our resignation and expressing thanks and gratitude for our old company's support over the years. This is a great time to acknowledge those who have helped us grow and develop. Even if we have issues with our old company, using our notice as an opportunity to give negative feedback could poison our opportunity to work with these same people in the future. If asked, we can selectively offer suggestions for improvement, but we need to avoid overt negative comments.

- How do we manage a counter-offer? I find ten percent of the candidates I work with receive a counter-offer and ninety percent of this group will decline the offer. In general, a company counters with more money, a promotion, or an offer for a larger role in the future. Accepting any kind of counter-offer always begs the question: why they did not offer us this before we gave notice? It can also leave seeds of doubt in the minds of our colleagues or supervisors that we are at high risk for leaving in the future if something else comes along. People who accept a counter-offer are more likely to leave within the first few years because even with a promotion or more money, the company culture and the various opportunities and challenges usually change very little. Of course, there are exceptions when staying makes sense and our company presents us with a truly exceptional opportunity.

- As we consider our new opportunity, we should ask ourselves about our overall impression of the new organization. Most people want to take pride in their company. If this is important to us, we need to ask, "Do they have a high level of integrity and standards? Does their reputation indicate they value their employees and the community as a whole?"

- Is our new company too good to be true? Does this new job appear easy and are the expectations of the managers modest? Have we been overly impressed with how nice the people are, how perfect their product works, or how convenient this job will be? I personally accepted a job years ago with a widely respected firm, but then found out they had some major manufacturing problems and were going through a product recall. My manager was difficult and was let go several months later. Too late, I realized I did not complete sufficient due diligence before accepting the position and instead was dazzled by the company's name and their quick market penetration.

- Is the management team sharp, supportive, and focused on mentoring their employees? There are several things to consider here. The first is we need to ask ourselves if we observed a strong sense of employee supportiveness in the interview process. If we did not, why would we expect this after they hire us? This should be a red flag. The second issue is even if we see a lot of support, this support may not continue. We need to keep in mind that we are being recruited; therefore, we are seeing the best face of the company. We need to look beyond the niceties to sort out the truth by asking others and investigating further. Determining the supportive nature of a company and its employees can be difficult and generally comes from networking with others, including current employees and ex-employees. We must do our best to avoid difficult managers or company cultures that can negatively—and significantly—influence our job satisfaction.
- Is this new job at least an incremental improvement over what we have done in the past? We want to look for something that adds value like better technology, more responsibility, future growth opportunities or an improved working environment. The work should be stimulating, challenging and allow us to grow with our new role. Otherwise, why would we leave our old job?

- Salary and benefits are logistics and not something that stimulates, challenges, nurtures or develops us as people. We all need money to take care of families, our different lifestyles and ourselves. Yes, we want to assure ourselves that we can meet our financial needs, but a career is more than simply a financial transaction. As we spend a great deal of time at work, we want our job to be a generally positive and exciting component of our lives. I wrote about this earlier.

The final point is that we can walk away if the job is not a good fit. To do otherwise is a poor decision. Ideally, we should constantly be working on self-improvement: developing new skills, increasing knowledge, and building our character. We are thus a valuable employee and should be confident in saying no to a less-than-ideal job opportunity, as we can expect another one—a better one—in the near future.

Chapter 7: Why Did We Not Get the Job?

Unfortunately, we went through the entire interview process and did not get the job. Even if we are not certain we would have accepted the job, it can still be deflating to be turned down for the position. However, there is always value in analyzing our interview experiences and learning from them.

The following is a partial list of common reasons why companies turn down interviewed candidates:

- There was a stronger candidate with a better track record of performance. They scored higher on a SPEARS analysis, with more relevant experience and superior quantifiable performance. In response to this, we can gain more work experience and continue to work on our performance for the future.

- As I wrote about in a previous chapter, failure to prepare is the number one preventable mistake in not getting an offer. To remedy this, we can work on improving our interviewing skills, learn more about the company, understand how our skills and experiences relate to the job, and present our authentic self in the most convincing manner. This also includes being on time for the interview, dressing well, and bringing along a well-thought-out business plan or resume as needed.

- We failed to ask good questions of the interviewer. Our questions were not as articulate and thoughtful as they could be. We missed the opportunity to demonstrate we did our homework and understood both the company and our possible role.

- We failed to listen. Some candidates are so busy trying to make their case and talk about what *they* think is important, that they forget to listen. They do not allow the interviewer to drive the process; instead, they gloss over the interviewer's questions and focus on their own agenda. While we should always have a game plan when we interview, we need to remember we are not in the driver's seat. The interviewer wants to see how we adapt in a situation where we do not have control. Our failure to listen is a major concern for many managers. If we cannot listen in an interview, why should they expect us to listen if they hire us?

- As a follow-up to the previous point, there are some people who talk too much in an interview. This is not just failing to listen; this is excessive, unfocused, non-pertinent chatter. While this might be part of someone's personality, it also is likely a result of nervousness or uncertainty in the candidate. There are two simple solutions: role-play an interview with someone we know, to garner more experience and feedback for improvement; and/or spend more time preparing so we are more confident. We want to come across as steady and centered in the interview, not nervous and uncertain.

- Overt lying or even little white lies have no place on the resume. The most common omissions are people trying to cover up time gaps in their resume, their lack of a college degree, a DUI, or the lack of performance data. They might intentionally leave out certain information or massage the resume so it is more difficult to discern the facts. A good interviewer will uncover these issues through detailed questioning.

- I observe ten to twenty cases per year of people eliminated from the interview process by evasiveness. They may have been humiliated or embarrassed about some of their past poor decisions or mistakes but their evasiveness made it worse. This does not mean we should data-dump all of our foibles and career mistakes during the interview, but honesty and straightforwardness about our resume or in response to a direct question is required.

- Some candidates try to answer questions when they have no idea what they are talking about. *It is better to answer a question with "I do not know" then to make things up.* We can tell the interviewer, "This is my best guess although I am not certain" or "I do not know the answer but I can do some research and get back to you later." Admitting a lack of knowledge is far better than trying to act knowledgeable on a subject we know little about. We end up spewing forth superfluous information that makes us look silly.

- Companies hire to fulfill their needs; thus, we must properly inquire about what is important to them. Some candidates fail to ask the interviewer what the critical aspects of the job are and what they can do as an employee to accomplish the necessary tasks in a timely manner.

Make Your Career Meaningful: A Practical Toolbox

- Normally a company will interview multiple people for a given role. We need to find a way to differentiate ourselves from the rest of the candidates. While this may occur automatically if we have a better SPEARS profile, it behooves us to look further at our various skills and credentials that might separate us from the pack. If we review the backgrounds of the people we will be interviewing with, can we find some common threads of experience? In doing our homework, have we uncovered any pertinent information related to the products or services of the company that we can share with the interviewer? Or perhaps as we were checking out their company, we talked to some potential customers and generated a few leads that the company might find beneficial. I can recall a sales candidate talking to a potential customer and actually picking up a sizeable purchase order that he then took to the interview. Needless to say, he got the job. He clearly differentiated himself from the other candidates.

- Some people come into the interview with an entitled attitude. This is a blend of overconfidence and hubris that says, "I am well-qualified for this role, have the right background and therefore SHOULD be hired." When these people do not get the job, they tend to respond with angry indignation and accuse the company of being "blind." This arrogance generally leaks out in the interview and leads to a resounding, "No!" from the interviewer. The company is looking for people who are confident and skilled—not people who think they have all the answers and have nothing more to learn.

- Employers are looking for a candidate who has a good story and can articulate in concise and thoughtful terms what they can offer and how they work together with others. They are looking for communicators. Indeed, excellent communication is a crucial criterion for many customer-facing employees. The lack of an articulate career story comes across negatively in an interview. Thus, it is imperative that a candidate have a clear idea of their own story. We must be able to answer questions about ourselves in a concise, yet well-thought-out manner. We can use a SPEARS analysis and an LPV to help formulate our story.

- "Low energy" and "lack of enthusiasm" are two frequently mentioned reasons why people do not receive an offer. Many interviewers are expecting candidates to come in with energy and enthusiasm. We cannot convert our Type B personality to a Type A personality, but we can engage the interviewer with great eye contact, questions, a good story and a keen focus of attention.

- Interviewers expect prompt follow-up from the candidate through some sort of thank you. This note should express gratitude for the interviewer's time, a few statements about the interview, how the candidate is a good fit for the role, and a clear interest in moving forward in the interview process. Frequently, I hear concerns from an interviewer or company that a candidate has not followed up after the interview. We must write a thank you note *on the same day* of the interview. Another point to remember is that some managers are very meticulous about proper grammar and spelling so we must carefully proofread our writing before sending it off.
- Unrealistic salary and benefits requirements represent a small percentage of the candidates I see rejected for an offer. They are asking for compensation well outside of the norm for the company or they are looking for a huge increase beyond their current level of compensation.
- Bad-mouthing our old company is unacceptable. This is almost always perceived as whining and complaining and is a strong turn off. As I wrote in an earlier chapter, even if the facts are true and our old company was a mess, this is not the time or place to complain.
- Pessimism is a major turn-off. This is a blind spot for many people because pessimism is

often a protective mechanism that speaks of a history of disappointment. A pessimist's best attempt to be cheerful, upbeat, and sincere in their statements will fail. The underlying chip on the shoulder, cynicism, and know-it-all nature comes through in body language, tone of voice, eye contact (or lack of it) and the type of responses the candidate makes. Some people truly do not know themselves very well or are not willing to put in the self-reflective work get to know themselves better. Others fail to understand that most people are not interested in working with self-indulgent, disorganized, whiny and complaining people. The solution to this problem? A lot of personal work, which will be written about in later chapters.

- There are other reasons people are not hired. They dress inappropriately or look disheveled in their hair or grooming. The rule is to always overdress for an interview, be early, do not have hair in your face, get a haircut, and iron your suit. Also, avoid being controversial with non-work-related issues.

- Some hiring managers, especially those in sales or marketing, expect us to ask for objections and concerns and close the interview aggressively. (This was discussed in detail in an earlier chapter.) Failure to do so in certain job interviews will result in elimination as a candidate.

- Finally, we can be knocked out of the interview process through a bad reference. Perhaps the interviewers know someone we used to work with, called him without our knowledge, and got a bad reference. We are unlikely to even know this has happened and thus cannot address the issue directly.

I can recall several managers refusing to consider well-qualified candidates because of things that occurred more than ten years ago, frequently a personal interaction rather than poor performance on the job. I remember one senior manager receiving a poor reference of "incompetence" for a candidate. It turns out the reference was holding a long-standing grudge on the candidate from years before when this candidate refused to support a business decision put forth by the reference. The candidate made the right call, but the reference never forgave him.

The lesson learned is to never burn bridges and always behave professionally, even if those around us do not. In addition, if we offer references to the hiring company, we must know in advance how our references will speak about us. Yes, I have listened to many poor references supplied by the candidates themselves. Unfortunately, these candidates fail to understand how they present to others and are unaware of how their references will speak about them. Life is complex, we all make mistakes, and some people are very unforgiving. We cannot control what other people do or say about us but we can always try to do our best and uphold our own high standards.

Chapter 8: We Got the Job, Now What?

We have received the job offer, accepted the job, given notice at our old company, and are starting at our new company this week. Should we have a plan in place for our new job? Yes. The new company will dictate our key functions, responsibilities, interactions, and workflow, but here are a few thoughts we should also consider.

We are no longer with any of our previous companies. We are with a new company; to quote Dorothy from the Wizard of Oz, "We are not in Kansas anymore." The rules have changed and we will be confronted with new challenges and issues. There is nothing wrong with applying the great skills we have developed over the years to our new job. That is part of the reason we were hired. But we must be fully conscious that the new company may respond to us in a dramatically different way than our old company. This is because we are surrounded by a unique mix of new people and circumstances. I have many examples of people moving from Company A to Company B and becoming frustrated because their actions did not get the responses they expected. They blamed the company, but the truth is they had failed to prepare themselves to accept the newness of their situation. We must embrace the challenges and excitement of working in a different environment with new people.

It is very common for people, especially experienced ones, to come into a new company and set up shop like they have in the past. This includes everything from the pictures they place on their desk, to their mannerisms, to how they organize their day. I call this process "nesting" and it reminds me of how animals frequently set up their personal space. For example, my dog Gracie approaches her dog pillow, scratches and pokes around a bit with her snout, turns around three times and then plops down. She has now created a comfortable place where she can rest or look around. Most people do the same thing in their office, creating a "nest" that is familiar and comfortable to them.

We also might extend this "nest" outside of our personal office and use the same communication skills and familiar ideas in our new job. Once again, we need to realize this is a new place and our habitual behaviors may not serve us well with our new employer. We need to proceed with caution and learn the new customs and idiosyncrasies of our new environment.

Our new place of employment becomes an excellent opportunity to develop new knowledge and work-related skills while building strong business relationships. This relates to the letter "E" (Education) in a SPEARS analysis as we learn to adjust to new surroundings. In addition to all the training a new company has to offer, the following are some other ideas to consider as a part of this education process.

Relationships

Some people fail to focus on their new business relationships. A new company requires a fresh look at how to effectively communicate, integrate and create productive relationships.

- Working and building relationships takes a lot of time and effort. It is more than simple niceties and cordiality. No matter what our role is in the company, we must take the time to build this bridge with our colleagues and associates. Building great relationships includes many qualities such as listening, respect, helpfulness, patience, loyalty, a common purpose, and a willingness to share skills, knowledge, and expertise. This is a continual process and is not accomplished in a few days, weeks or months.

- The most important issue when it comes to relationships is our desire to build one. Many people say, "I am who I am" and expect others to accept who they are. They place minimal effort in building a strong connection with their fellow workers. After an initial flurry of niceties to establish some type of relationship, they quit feeding the relationship. *It is like planting a garden, watching the seeds sprout, and then discontinuing all watering, fertilizing and weeding.* The net effect is that over time the plants will die off and we will be left with the "psychological weeds" of distrust, unresolved conflicts and anger. Our bridge of professional relationships is a large part of our work environment and must be cultivated.

- New Year's Resolutions tend to be short-lived. They go by the wayside when we become fatigued, frustrated, or fail to see the positive impact of our efforts. Productive work relationships, like New Year's Resolutions, will challenge us to stay the course. This is especially true when the road gets rough and we experience the potholes of difficult people and challenging circumstances. We need to exercise self-discipline and patience as we continue our efforts to work productively with others, regardless of the situation.

- There is the issue of bringing our home life into the office. Have you ever observed others coming to the office when they are clearly working through emotional or mental distress? Most people are unlikely to discuss personal issues with colleagues or associates to gain support or understanding. Thus, we may give off the impression that we are either chronically moody or upset. We can effectively manage this by compartmentalizing our emotions or distressful thoughts. We do this all the time by exercising self-control over what is appropriate behavior or not for a given situation. For example, we know to be quiet in a library, meeting or classroom setting. Or, we know how to be courteous and polite as we greet people in a formal setting.

We can do the same thing with work—we can exercise self-control and restraint while at work and hold our moodiness in check. Clearly, we cannot do this indefinitely—if our home problems are chronic, we need to take appropriate action to remedy the situation.

- We all have biases, preferences, pre-conceived ideas, and strong beliefs. *Are our biases interfering with our ability to be a better manager, individual contributor or executive?* Do we even know what our biases are?

Some of our biases are healthy, such as those in favor of integrity, gratitude, forgiveness, productivity, or understanding. On the other hand, we have negative biases, too: for example, that there are only certain ways to do things, that we are always right, that the input of others is not that important, or that there is only one right answer to a problem. How many times have you thought that someone else in the office is exceptionally rigid and married to his or her bad habits? If this thought has indeed crossed your mind, it is probable that others have thought the same towards you.

Make Your Career Meaningful: A Practical Toolbox

- One of the easiest ways to identify a negative bias is to look at those situations at work that create the most angst in us. This indicates we have "hit a nerve" and stumbled upon a strong belief or bias that is pushing our buttons. We might equate it with needing to be in control, expecting perfection of ourselves, feeling impatient with others or harboring unrealistic expectations. We need to let go of our unhealthy biases, or we are destined to be miserable every time they come up. I will write about this further in a later chapter.

- We have now arrived at our new company and have brought our entire personality and skill set with us, warts and all. As we work on learning new things, this is also the opportunity to evaluate ourselves and chose what we want to discard. Over the years we have probably learned a lot about what does not work in the workplace, including a know-it-all attitude, overzealous nature, impatience, anger, lack of respect for others, and poor listening skills. Now we can ask ourselves, "What have I learned from the past that did not work well and I am ready to let go of? If it is a personality issue with how I relate to others, how can I change this or exercise better self-control so this does not happen again?" This type of self-evaluation and removal of our psychological garbage will pay major dividends in the future.

- A detailed game plan on how to create outstanding relationships is a book in itself and beyond the scope of this chapter. Hopefully, you will recognize the necessity of work in this area and explore it further. A key part of building relationships starts with working within ourselves and identifying our issues of anger, fear, guilt, damaging beliefs along with building our qualities of character. I will write about this more in later chapters.

Business Knowledge and Skills

- Each day brings new opportunities to learn and extract lessons and ideas from various experiences. Commonly, people assume that each day is like another, just "the same old stuff." This belief shuts down the possibility of new perceptions or sensory input. The exception to this is when we are exposed to new situations or experiences, like a new job.

As an example, have you ever driven into a new city where you did not know the terrain, streets or buildings? Did you notice how you were acutely aware of what was going on and paid close attention to everything around you? The same can be said when you meet interesting people for the first time. You might glom on to their every word as you decipher what they are saying and try to put the person and their ideas into perspective.

On the other hand, what about driving the same road every day and meeting the same people? Do you notice how you are not as attentive or focused and take many things for granted? The same is true at work. We may start off more attentive but eventually we assume it is always "the same old stuff" and we shut down any new input.

The truth is, if we pay attention, things are changing all the time! Yes, gradual day-to-day change is often a slower process than the stark contrast of moving to a totally new environment, but it is still present. We must learn to not take things for granted, even after we have been in our job for a long while. *How many times in your career have you assumed something and found it not to be true?* This could be when you started with a new company, assumed things would function in a certain way, and they did not. Or, perhaps it was a situation you had experienced many times before and assumed you had it figured out and missed that something had changed. The point to remember is this: cultivating the habit of intense observation and curiosity is the hallmark of highly successful and creative people. They assume less and look for what is different or has changed. Do you take the time to do this on a regular basis?

- While every day brings a chance to learn something new by observing our surroundings, we also have the opportunity to "sharpen our swords" or business skills and acumen. This is a daily attempt to exercise our business related muscles through study, practice, observation, contemplation and analysis. The best executives make it a point to review their work regularly, figure out what went right or wrong, and why. Furthermore, they do this without prejudice, guilt, anger or fear. A non-confrontational internal dialogue explores and evaluates the day without condemning and criticizing.

- Most people, especially new employees, are interested in company training. We want to assure ourselves that we have the tools and support to succeed in our new role, and thus should take advantage of all training programs within the company. However it is equally important that we take ownership of our training and consider this to be as much our responsibility as the company's responsibility. How can we take ownership? We can continually pepper colleagues and associates with questions about best practices and different ways to approach the work. We can take home extra reading material and explore new ideas on the Internet. If we do not understand something or seem to be unable to make adequate progress, we can reach out for help. Some people feel embarrassed when things do not come quickly or easily, and take their lack of progress as a reason to isolate themselves from those who can help. However, this is the very worst thing we can do in this situation. Instead, we must reach out to others, take personal responsibility for our training, and refrain from relying fully on the company.

Chapter 9: Better Ways to Manage Our Anger, Fear and Guilt

What do anger, fear and guilt have to do with developing a meaningful and successful career? Anger, fear, and guilt are just part of the human condition. Why not accept and live with these feelings? These are good points and the following material will give us some perspectives to consider.

Finding better ways to manage our anger, fear and guilt can significantly help with our careers. For example, what happens if we have a disagreement with our boss or colleague, or a client thinks our services were unsatisfactory, or we failed to adequately prepare for a meeting? These types of events are likely to occur for all of us at some point. We will likely respond with negative emotions that over time can dampen our enthusiasm, productivity and relationships.

In order to work with anger, guilt, or fear, we must first acknowledge we have a problem. Most people rarely admit or think of themselves as hostile, moody, irritable, fearful or shameful. While some might admit to occasional outbursts of irritation, they genuinely feel they are pleasant to be around; if they are upset, they think they have good reasons to feel this way.

In order to truly see our outward expressions of negative emotions as damaging to both our personal welfare and the welfare of others, we must stop denying our negativity. We must stop rationalizing it with the easy excuse that, if we feel angry or anxious, this is a "normal" response to our situation. Indeed, there are alternative ways to behave instead of getting upset. *We must also see past the idea that we will always be at least mildly irritable, fearful, or guilt-ridden.* We can do better! We can actually *change* our emotional responses.

In order to see how we really behave, we can ask ourselves a few simple questions:

- Do we constantly fret about our job?
- Is our daily mood normally light, joyful and easy, or intense and anxious?
- Are we unforgiving to ourselves when we fail to achieve a goal?

- Are we constantly frustrated with our progress?
- Do we worry about our next work disaster even when things are going well?
- Do we have recurring irritating issues with our boss or colleagues?
- Do we get upset and think others take advantage of us?
- Do we tend to put people off or see them as incompetent, inferior or stupid?
- Are headaches and backaches common for us?
- Do little problems in the office bug us?
- Do we tend to overreact?
- Are we constantly measuring and judging others, including ourselves?
- Do we spend time reliving and talking with others about old wounds from our work life?

If the answer is yes to some of these questions, we might have a problem with our emotional responses to events.

Furthermore, our emotional issues can become chronic. For example, we are anxious about completing a work project but eventually we succeed. We experience a momentary sense of relief—but soon our anxiety returns, as we wonder if our boss will accept the work. Eventually he does and we relax, but our worry returns as we contemplate presenting this to a group and anticipating their response. As it turns out, our project is great but our boss gives us a new project and our anxiety or fear starts over again. The cycle repeats itself and it is one anxiety after another that never ends. On a deeper level, we are in a constant state of trying to do a great job, be accepted by others, and not make any mistakes. At the end of the day, there is a never-ending need to be the *perfect little employee* and that is impossible.

Some people may exhibit outward self-control (remain calm and polite in demeanor) but in fact be simmering on the inside with anger, guilt and fear. While pretending to handle life with ease can be useful socially, it does not negate the damage done by the bottled-up internal turmoil. This just buries the stress deeper, making everything worse, and can lead to other pathologies like passive-aggressive behavior, depression, generalized anxiety disorder or physical ailments.

Working on mental and emotional health is not a passive process or a "quick fix." There are many ingrained habits in us that are resistant to change. They are the bodyguards that protect our outdated behavior and responses to life while making it difficult to improve our character and develop better self-control. *The goal to working with anger, fear, and guilt is to moderate them, bring them under better control, and thereby minimize their ability to create havoc in our work or personal life.*

Anger, fear, and guilt are all responses to a threat. When the threat seems stronger than we are, or we perceive it as overwhelming and unfair, we often resort to fear and anger or a mixture of both. Guilt occurs when we somehow assume we are at fault for the situation or should have been smart or strong enough to have prevented it or reversed it once it started.

This parallels the common statement that there are only three basic ways to cope with any threat: fight, flight, or freeze. An appropriate translation of these would be: fight equals an *angry* response; flight is a response of *fear*; and freezing in place is what happens when we paralyze ourselves with *guilt*. While some people might think there is little we can do to manage these dark moods, the truth is that we can work to drastically reduce these destructive emotional responses.

Most of our emotional responses have their origin in our youth and were the tools we used to survive. They were our full repertoire of ways to fight danger when we were small and unsophisticated. However, these basic responses are outdated and no longer necessary. Furthermore, these behaviors have not only outlived their usefulness, they are now a determent to mature adult living.

Working on our difficult emotional responses can also improve our health. We all have a mind-body connection and our exposure to chronic mental and emotional distress can lead to muscle aches, backaches, headaches, and bellyaches in addition to a lowered immune response.

Medication, meditation, biofeedback, mindfulness, yoga, acupuncture, chiropractic care, exercise and counseling are reasonable tools to employ to help manage our damaging emotional responses. In this chapter, I will offer up some cognitive ideas and approaches as one option to deal with these difficulties.

Fear

Fear is not something we either can or wish to fully eliminate from our lives. Fear can function well as a healthy caution, calling attention to potentially dangerous situations. However, in its extreme or chronic form, it is excessive and destructive.

Managing fear requires us to set up an internal dialogue between our mature adult self and our youthful outdated ideas of how to respond to life. Our approach is to upgrade our old habits of responding to life and we do this with compassion and thoughtfulness. We work through this upgrade in our minds using the following steps:

- This internal dialogue in our minds must be respectful and understanding while eliminating all self-effacing or derogatory comments like stupid, dumb or idiot.

- We need to understand that we are educating this angry, fearful or guilty part of ourselves to adopt a more intelligent version of protecting ourselves that incorporates additional wisdom and skills. To be concerned about threats to our well-being is good, but we must express these concerns in a more effective and healthy way.

- We must first ask ourselves to reduce our fearful or angry responses. A primal part of us responds to danger, and we need to coax it to relax its aggressive fearful or angry habit. We want to create a relationship like a parent to a child, with the parent possessing greater wisdom, compassion, and authority.

Ultimately, the youthful fearful (or angry/guilty) part of us needs to understand and embrace adult rules and strategies as the new standard for healthy living.

- We must then have a conversation with ourselves while imparting wisdom and perspective. Some of our dialogue might include the following questions:
  - Are the specifics of what happened to us important enough to warrant an emotional outburst?
  - Do we constantly have to focus on who "did this" to us, why we have to deal with this, or where this hurt originated?
  - Are we failing to recognize that it is impossible to control everything and have it all work out perfectly?
  - Can we see that others have issues too; it is not just all about us?
  - Do we fail to realize that our life is part of something larger and there is more complexity than we readily see?
  - When we really think about it, is the motivating force that recreates fear, anger or guilt some irrational or silly problem that has long since vanished?
  - Even if it is a big issue like a major battle with our boss or a pending company layoff, does our fear or anger improve

the situation or can we use the time to investigate future options and solutions?

o Do we fail to recognize that as an adult, we can be active in dealing with difficult situations far beyond just becoming emotionally upset?

Even after having this rational conversation with ourselves, we might find that our fearful, angry or guilty responses continue. *This is due to our long-term habit of excessive emotional responses that is almost like an addiction. Breaking this habit takes time and regular effort.*

In working with all of these negative emotional responses, this must be more than a one-time effort. We might spend a few minutes each day and go through any challenging issues that overwhelm us. We can ask ourselves, "Could I have handled this differently with less emotional involvement?" or "What new perspectives can I use to calm my childish anger, fear or guilt?" This is our mature adult self taking control of how we respond to life's challenges.

Anger

Excessive anger, like fear, is another response to life issues that we developed in our youth and never modified. We can try to reduce its impact using the same type of cognitive dialogue as described above for fear.

This angry protective part of us fights for what it wants (whether deserved or not). *This anger not only attacks perceived physical dangers of potential violence or loss of home or family, but also psychological dangers of humiliation, embarrassment, loss of opportunity, failure, and regret.*

One can argue that all of these issues are valid and it would be acceptable to be angry or irritated by them. While it might seem sensible to be angry in these situations, the anger does not help resolve any issues or bring us peace of mind. On the plus side, anger can give us added strength if we need it to protect ourselves in a life-threatening situation, but this is extremely rare.

Some believe we must express our anger because unexpressed anger may harm us by denying our feelings. In learning more positive ways to deal with anger, we are not denying our feelings but instead are listening to their messages and choosing to respond differently. This does not mean we become a victim and do nothing. When we notice a rising irritation over an event, this is a time to take action to correct or relieve the issue. We can stand up for ourselves and work to resolve issues, but we can do so in a calm, intelligent and thoughtful manner, without anger. Doing so also tends to yield better results than lashing out in angry tirades. *We also need to stop spending time contemplating other people who might have been overly punitive to us in the distant past.* Reliving old or even more recent hurts makes us feel worse and does not solve the problems of today.

There used to be a popular method of *letting it all out* by blasting our anger out at others, beating up a pillow, or yelling at the universe. This self-indulgent program advised that screaming our anger towards anyone we felt deserved it was the best form of treatment. By doing this, we would clear away all of our pent-up, angry baggage. However, this *letting it all out* tool was ineffective. While some people experienced short-term relief due to the exhilaration of appearing to defeat their enemies, the main experiences were exhaustion and the alienation of others.

Guilt

Guilt is an experience of embarrassment, self-loathing, humiliation, and unworthiness because we have failed to live up to certain criteria. In simple terms, we feel guilty by failing to live up to some standards set by ourselves or possibly by others.

There are two ideas to consider when working with guilt. The first point is to evaluate the standard we have set for our self and determine if it is reasonable.

The second issue is managing the rigidity and intensity with which we discipline ourselves for failing to achieve this standard.

People can experience guilt as they try to live up to unrealistic levels of achievement and rigid standards as the basis for their self-worth. Their inner-critic is overactive, too intense, and even tyrannical. *It demands unreasonable standards, which repeatedly sets us up to "fix the unfixable" and "cure the incurable"—a recipe for disaster!* These unrealistic expectations are likely our youthful attempt to please others and be accepted (usually by authority figures). Ideally, as we grow older, we should re-evaluate these standards—but unfortunately, many of us do not.

So how do we re-evaluate any ridiculous internal standards that are unachievable and result in guilt? We can have an intelligent conversation with ourselves as we did with anger and fear to establish control over any overzealous desires to achieve unrealistic standards.

Anytime we experience excessive guilt, we can ask ourselves, "What is the standard we have failed to live up to?" or "Can we reasonably live up to this standard or ideal?" In addition, if we have not met the standards, we can ask ourselves, "Am I being reasonable in disciplining myself? Will this motivate me to achieve these standards?"

For example, our boss could give us a goal that is impossible to achieve, we fail to meet it, and thus we experience excessive guilt. We need to realize the goal was unachievable, release the internal guilt, and approach our boss to discuss his unrealistic expectations, or consider other methods to manage this issue without guilt.

Some people might argue that guilt is necessary because a good dose of guilt makes us more self-examined and keeps us on the "straight and narrow." However, strong and constant guilt, just like strong and constant anger or fear, is destructive as it tears us down and damages our ability to experience a healthy sense of self-worth.

Another issue with guilt is that it does not guarantee we will do anything to remedy our behavior. For example, we could be an obnoxious and difficult person, feel guilty but never do anything to fix ourselves. *People can be sorry for what they have done but never do anything to change their behavior or try to make amends.* They believe that being sorry or feeling guilty is punishment enough.

Another scenario we need to manage is if we either violate our own or others' reasonable standards. This means the standards were reasonable but we failed to live up to them. Does this mean it is now okay to feel exceptionally guilty? A better solution is to use the experience of our failure to learn and improve our skills and knowledge so we can do better next time. We might have violated a reasonable standard such as failing to be kind and thoughtful to others, finishing our work or meeting reasonable goals. We can strive to improve ourselves by asking others for help, making amends, learning new skills or and taking responsibility for our actions. By doing all of these things, we are less likely to repeat our errors. This is a far better approach then just feeling guilty.

The following are several other examples to illustrate some of the above ideas.

1. *We are disappointed and experience guilt because we think we let down a significant client. We perceive the client is dissatisfied with our performance and feel we failed to meet their standards.* In this situation, the client established a standard we did not achieve. We first must look at the standard that was established and ask if it was reasonable. If the standard was reasonable and we have failed to achieve success in the eyes of our client, this is the time to evaluate our process and skills. We need to ask ourselves questions such as:

- Was I caught by surprise and did not anticipate problems?
- What are the skills I need to acquire to improve my performance, and how do I develop these skills?
- Do I have an issue with communication? Would better communication have garnered a better result?
- Have I set up unrealistic expectations with my process?
- Who can I approach to gather better ideas and tools to help me in the future?

The idea is to probe and understand what we can do to improve ourselves and then take action. This reduces the chances of failure in the future. We can also make amends through apologizing, trying to remedy the situation, and reinforcing our commitment to serving the client.

2. *We feel disappointed with ourselves because we failed to achieve the goals we set for ourselves. We are angry and ashamed by our lack of achievement.* Once again, we can ask ourselves about our standards and expectations. Were our goals reasonable and achievable? We can then ask ourselves the following questions:

- It all starts with defining objectives. What are our goals? Are they qualities of character like courage, stamina, or perseverance? Alternatively, are they skills such as organizing our day, managing clients, or handling our team?

- Our ability to persist even when our mind is less enthusiastic takes commitment and self-control. Have we reminded ourselves why we are doing this to begin with? Do we see the value in our efforts?

- We want to make sure we have isolated and targeted the areas we want to develop. Are our efforts too general or too grand in scope?

- We might experience additional obstacles such as fatigue or resistance. Does our project seem too difficult? To help us move forward, we can draw strength from recognizing the meaningfulness of accomplishing the goal.

- There may be times when we become discouraged because we see no progress. We need to look for help in getting us through these "deserts" of no results. Can we improve our faith in ourselves by observing that others have been down this path before and succeeded?

- Have we asked others for input and determined that the goals set were achievable if we allotted more time for them? Do we have an issue with patience?
- Are there more skills required? If so, what are they?

We need to realize our excessive reactions of guilt, anger or fear hold no power over us unless we let them. If we continue to see these emotions as terrible and difficult to manage, they will remain significant in our daily experiences. Yet if we can see them for what they are—our youthful attempts to manage a complex life and an inability to come up with more mature options—we are better able to modify our behavior.

Managing Critical People

Managing critical people is a special problem and can invoke fear, anger and guilt. Most people struggle with criticism because they interpret it as a failure and not a learning experience. Some of us take this further and assume we have not just made a mistake but that we ourselves *are* a mistake. We need to find a more intelligent approach to handling criticism, how we perceive making mistakes and what we can learn from these experiences.

Some people use the dark side of criticism—to humiliate, embarrass, degrade, and control others. If we recognize this is happening, we need to use our discerning skills to protect ourselves against this type of overzealous attack.

Too much criticism, or our poor response to criticism, can damage us. We can overcompensate and become too agreeable, too forgiving, and too helpful, thereby letting ourselves be exploited. Criticism can invalidate us by making us feel inferior, inadequate, ignorant, insensitive, or lacking in responsibility. We miss opportunities and belittle our ability to contribute. Criticism may morph into a strong inner critic, constantly berating ourselves, making us feel alienated and worthless.

Some difficult people take on the role of an invalidator. They do their dirty deeds by trying to confuse us or make it seem like everything is our fault. They may falsely accuse us, exaggerate small problems, and then attack our character instead of the issue. With these types of people, we first need to check their motives before we check ourselves. We need to halt our initial response of trying to figure out where we screwed up. Instead, we need to consider whether this critical and invalidating person communicates this way on a regular basis. If so, it is not our problem—it is theirs.

When we must work with such critical people, we need to:

- Stay calm, listen carefully and ask questions to find solutions. Do not let the person push us down the path of thinking it is our fault.
- Understand that even if we make mistakes, we must recognize partial successes versus "complete failures" in what we do.
- Judge each event on its own merits versus lumping them all together. Failing one time does not make us a failure.
- Avoid seeing things as unchangeable or permanent. There will be new opportunities in the future and we need to prepare ourselves for when they come about.
- Be careful not to overextend ourselves. There are times that we will attempt to do too much in order to please others.
- Give ourselves some level of control; otherwise, we will miss many opportunities. We need to see ourselves as in control of our lives.
- Stop obsessing about the situation and learn to focus on the moment.

- Make sure we do not expect more of the same—more problems, negativity and disappointment. We need to relax in the idea that our days are not all "doom and gloom." There will be good times ahead as there have been in the past.

By combining all of these tools and working on them regularly, we are in a better position to handle the critical person in our midst.

There are times when the overly critical person is correct and we have made a mistake. We need to decide whether the standards from which they measured are reasonable. If we think they are and we have not measured up, then we can work on new skills and gain knowledge in order to do better next time. *The important point is that WE, not the overly critical person, are the ones to determine the validity of the standards. Frequently, their standards are unrealistic or intended to harm, not help.*

We also want to reframe criticism. It is not meant to be a vehicle to nit-pick everything that went wrong, establish blame, and persecute the guilty—not unless our intent is to humiliate, eliminate, or control others. Instead, we want to build something positive by becoming aware of what went wrong and how to fix it. Criticism can (and should!) be a constructive, useful learning process.

Will there come a time when we no longer need to manage our anger, fear, and guilt or deal with critical people? Not likely. The complexity of life will continue to challenge us as we take on new roles and responsibilities. Thus, our need for self-improvement and evaluation always continues.

This program of self-improvement and the management of anger, fear and guilt requires a proactive approach of developing specific strengths, giving suitable praise, and fostering encouragement. We are our own coach and cheerleader; we need to acknowledge our own progress while also being patient. It is important to remember that we have automatically used our old habits or anger, fear and guilt for many years and it will take time to build new ones. However, we can do it!

Chapter 10: Changing Dysfunctional Workplace Beliefs

Beginning in our youth, we create a variety of beliefs and rules. To make sense of the world, we mentally construct these beliefs that become the internal laws we live by. These include our beliefs about the physical laws in the universe as well as our psychological beliefs. Some of our beliefs are reasonable and healthy, but others are toxic and lead us to despair, anger, guilt or fear. *Our beliefs are the tinted glasses we use to view our world and we must evaluate and correct them as necessary. They frequently create and reinforce our mental and emotional distress. For example, an early bad experience with an authority figure may lead us to believe we must be fearful and intimidated by those in charge.* Our beliefs actively participate in sustaining distress even when the scenario has passed. The good news: we can identify and change these beliefs and improve our well-being.

The following are a number of work-related beliefs that can lead to distressful responses. We might have created these, or similar beliefs, to cope with the world and their origins are not important. What is important is if they have outlived their usefulness and are no longer constructive to us.

When we are on autopilot—passive and giving little thought to our responses to life events—these negative habits or beliefs can take over. We need to:

- identify and understand our beliefs
- come up with a more mature belief to replace the old one, when necessary

Until we do, nothing will change. Once we recognize our negative beliefs, we can take charge of our responses to life, and thus open the door to beneficial changes.

Dysfunctional Beliefs

1) I am the only one who can have a bad day, not others.

We can become irritated or frustrated with others for their occasional moodiness and outbursts. Nobody enjoys being around people who are having a bad day. Their emotional behavior bothers us; we are busy enough without having to put up with their issues.

Yet we know that *life events* happen, frequently beyond our control. We all have issues and problems to manage: nobody is immune. It could be we have a sick child at home, had a fight with our spouse or missed a deadline at work. When it comes to our own problems, we expect others to respond with their full attention. We must be similarly sensitive to the problems and issues of others. Even when others lose self-control and lash out at us, we have probably been guilty of the same behaviors too at some point. Frequently, it is not a personal attack but instead a lack of self-control in managing being overwhelmed or stressed.

As mature adults, we can learn to manage our problems while reaching out for help when needed. We can learn to appreciate the issues of others and be helpful—as a minimum, we should be understanding. We do not have to fix the problems of other people, but we can be aware of their plight and relate to it. Thus, we can change our belief from, *"I am the only one who can have a bad day, not others"* to, *"Both others and myself have problems to manage that can overwhelm us, and I can be more understanding and helpful."*

2) Nobody trained me and therefore I have failed at work.

This toxic belief is our attempt to blame someone else for our failures when we do not want to blame ourselves. This also lets us off the hook for having to fix the problem because we did not create it, others did. We need to ask ourselves, is our role active or passive when it comes to work training? Can we take charge of our training by asking more questions and searching out other resources, or do we expect to be coddled?

The best approach to training is a combination of self-learning and taking full advantage of all of the company's resources. We are responsible for discussing with our employer what additional resources, information, and skills we need to acquire. They cannot read our minds or understand any of our unique learning issues unless we speak up. Thus, we can change the belief from, *"Nobody trained me so I have failed at work"* to, *"My training process is a joint effort between the company and me. I will take advantage of all their resources and seek out my own so I am knowledgeable and skilled about my role."*

3) I must do a perfect job and have all of the answers.

This is the belief of a perfectionist. While this goal is laudable, it is unattainable and will result in endless disappointments and discouragement. It does not take into account that a crucial part of the learning process is making mistakes and then modifying our actions or behaviors.

This belief can also lead to excessive concern to not humiliate or embarrass ourselves, as we are overly worried about what others think of us. The possibility of losing control and having others see us make mistakes can lead to a plethora of negative behaviors. For example, we might over-plan everything in minute detail, believing that through this, our work will progress effectively. We may hoard information or ideas, falsely believing that by having superior knowledge and solutions, we are indispensable and in-control. Or, we might become very defensive and defend our opinions aggressively. We perceive any opinion that does not agree with ours as a threat. We fight this threat by bullying others, and the result is that we further isolate ourselves.

Nobody is perfect. Nobody has all the answers or will never make mistakes. Our intense fear of humiliation and embarrassment is just an old, worn-out reaction that we can now eliminate. We are on a learning journey that will include mistakes as we encounter various complex issues. Thus we can change our old belief of, *"I must do a perfect job and have all of the answers"* to, *"I will do my best to learn, plan effectively, and perform well in my job. However, I will accept mistakes graciously, as part of my learning process, as I strive to do better."*

4) *Others do not treat me fairly at work.*

Often you might say to yourself or hear others say, "It's not fair." For example, we may not be promoted and think it is unfair—but in truth, we may not be the most qualified. Alternatively, we may be upset because others appear to receive better treatment from the boss, but they may be doing a better job than we are. Sometimes we may be blind to our own chronic "chip on the shoulder" pessimism, or a lack of sensitivity to others that alienates us. This can further reduce our opportunities for advancement or better treatment because we reap what we have sown.

On a broader scale, we might see our overall position in life as "unfair" because we are not as smart, creative, attractive, healthy, or dynamic as others are. In all these cases, we are focusing on what we do not have, where we have failed, and where we are lacking. Yet, everybody has areas of their life that need further development and refinement. Some people overcome their weak issues through hard work, but we must also realize there may be parts of life that we cannot change.

Some people think work is "unfair" because they do not feel respected. While everyone deserves respect as human beings, we generally earn respect in the workplace by our behavior, attitude, competence and thoughtfulness. We need to evaluate whether we have done these things to earn the respect of others and if we are treating others with respect, too. We must also learn to accept that regardless of how we behave, some people will support us while others will not.

We have a choice. Will we view the world as unfair and fill ourselves with anger and disappointment? On the other hand, we can accept our situation gracefully for those areas we cannot change, while working to build our strengths and do our best to improve. Thus we can change our belief from, *"Others do not treat me fairly at work"* to, *"I will sow the seeds of professionalism and competence and accept the things I cannot change."*

5) Others must do things my way or I get upset.

This belief says we expect others to work and behave in a certain way. In our minds, we have an ideal of how people should do their jobs; if they fail to live up to our ideal, we become frustrated and irritated. An example would be telling someone to file a stack of papers and insisting they follow a specific process. Alternatively, it could be giving a salesperson a list of goals and then spending time fussing about their process versus the results. It could be that we have expectations as to how people interact; we may favor an aggressive style versus a more thoughtful one. We could even extend our strong preferences to our homes where we expect others to do the dishes, mow the lawn, wash the car, or clean the bathroom in a particular way.

The common phrase used for this behavior is "micromanagement" and it relates to our insistence of a certain process versus a certain result. It is based upon our need to control and our own insecurities or fears. While we can all understand the importance of certain protocols in regulatory affairs, manufacturing, quality control or accounting, most roles have some level of flexibility.

Micromanagement creates stress as we fret about the actions of others, plus the negativity boomerangs back on us because most people resent this form of management. The scourge of micromanagement is not only applicable between an employee and their supervisor, but between colleagues too. While we may not have any authority over how other people do things, if their process continually bugs us we need to find better ways to manage our distress. *We can replace our old belief of, "Others must do things my way or I get upset"* with *"I expect a level of professionalism and results from a colleague or subordinate, but I can allow them to exercise an appropriate level of creativity or individualism."*

6) All I have to do is stay positive and everything will work out perfectly.

This belief states that by staying positive and continually reminding ourselves that we expect the best outcome, we will indeed experience the ideal result.

The idea of a positive thought is an alluring one because it is so simple. We just have to think this thought, fully act, speak and believe it, and we end up with what we want. This is a very attractive approach, but it is merely wishful thinking.

True, there is value in being optimistic, but we cannot succeed on optimism alone. We need to develop better skills and ideas, versus expecting that life will dump good results on us simply because we express positivity. For example, our work will not magically complete itself; we will not magically receive a promotion; and new clients will not magically appear unless we work hard to create this result.

Thus we can change this old belief of, *"All I have to do is stay positive and everything will work out perfectly"* to, *"I will use all of my skills and knowledge to achieve a good result while remaining optimistic that my efforts are supported."*

7) I should never ask questions because I might appear stupid or intimidate others.

Are we horrified when thinking of asking a question? This can be due to concerns that others will think our questions are stupid or that the person answering the question might become defensive. In either case, we can take the easy path and keep our mouths shut and allow this to inhibit our ability to learn.

We need to realize asking questions is more important than our concerns of humiliating ourselves or upsetting others. Have we considered that perhaps the person answering the question might learn something and others might benefit as well? Even if a few people think our questions are stupid or upsetting, we owe it to ourselves to gain clarity. Ultimately, our own growth and development as employees require inquiry and understanding. Thus, we can change our belief of, *"I should never ask questions because I might appear stupid or intimidate others"* to, *"Asking questions is how I learn. I need to ignore my fear of possible humiliation that interferes in my growth and development."*

8) I must always appear agreeable, not rock the boat or draw attention to myself.

This is our concern that if we point out a problem, others may view us as a complainer or we might offend someone. We must recognize that drawing attention to problems is critical to the growth of any company and ourselves. The company benefits by fixing the issue and we benefit by sharpening our analytical and discerning skills while becoming more valuable to the company.

Having others see us as a criticizer is usually the result of our attitude versus what we say. We can look inside ourselves and ask what motivates us to point out problems. Are we focused on helping others and our company, or do we simply relish being critical and humiliating our colleagues?

We can realize that it is normal to experience concern when a problem suddenly appears on the radar screen. Think about how we might respond to a flat tire, a failed project, a misunderstanding with a colleague, or an unexpected fight with our spouse. Nobody likes to deal with problems, but they are part of life. Problems do not usually go away on their own; they require attention and repair in order to move forward. Our boss or colleague may not jump for joy and thank us profusely when we point out a problem in their business plan but we owe it to them to share our knowledge so they can take the appropriate action. How we deliver the news is what makes it palatable. Do we point out problems with loathing and criticism, or with supportiveness and encouragement?

Thus, we can change our old belief of, *"I must always appear agreeable, not rock the boat or draw attention to myself"* to, *"I owe it to others to point out problems while maintaining my attitude of helpfulness, kindness and sensitivity."*

9) It is always about me.

We woke up this morning feeling anxious. The dog nips at us. Our boss makes a few snide remarks, and our colleagues seem more distant than usual. The first thought that may come to mind is, "It must be my fault and I did something wrong." Is it reasonable to blame ourselves for situations that do not seem to go our way?

One major reason we might think this way is failing to realize that other people have issues and problems of their own that are independent of us. They have their own lives, with their own personal challenges and career issues. They are likely doing their best, but perhaps their problems are causing a cascade of anger, fear, guilt, or sadness they are unable to control. This can affect their behavior, and we see the results through a variety of emotional outbursts.

It is important that we take time for self-evaluation to determine if we are unable to gracefully manage our daily challenges. But if we know that we are basically responsible and competent, yet continually blame ourselves for the rude or negative people in our lives, we need to rethink this assumption. We cannot be the scapegoat for all that is wrong around us. We must not take the moodiness, distress or bad behavior of others personally.

Realizing that everyone has issues makes us a more compassionate person. We must shoulder our own responsibilities and then we can potentially help others in their time of need. However, we need to recognize the world is complex with many people who have their own ideas, problems, emotional upsets, and ways of doing things.

We can be more understanding of others without accepting the burden of their problems and issues that have nothing to do with us. We can remain focused on managing ourselves and creating more harmony through our expressions of kindness, thoughtfulness, gratitude and patience. Thus, we can change our old belief from, *"It is always about me"* to, *"It is not always about me."*

Changing Our Destructive Beliefs

Working and changing our beliefs requires constant and regular effort, just like dealing with our anger, fear or guilt does. We must be firm and ready to dismiss our old destructive beliefs and to create healthy new beliefs. *We can remind ourselves of the many reasons why we no longer need to think this way, and remain diligent against using our old beliefs and behaviors "on autopilot."*

While there are destructive beliefs, we also possess healthy ones that support our career. These beliefs might focus on our qualities of gratitude, forgiveness, teamwork, kindness, competence, integrity, patience, self-control, perseverance and personal responsibility.

In order to let go of a distorted thought or belief, we must figure out what these beliefs are. What is the best way to identify a strong belief or dysfunctional thought? When we observe strong and powerful emotional responses to various scenarios, these are signals that we have stumbled upon a strong belief. The strongest and most powerful beliefs generally elicit the most aggressive mental or emotional reactions. Thus, as we go through our day and become particularly agitated by a work event, we must look for the belief associated with our response. The thought or belief comes first, followed by our emotional or mental reaction to it. The beliefs can be almost automatic, in fact so quick that we do not even notice them until we are already onto our emotional response. However, as we practice searching for these beliefs (by noting our strong emotional reactions to daily events) we will become more proficient at modifying destructive beliefs.

Does working with beliefs give us an instantaneous relief from our distress? While instant relief is possible, it usually takes time and repeated effort. We must be patient with ourselves as we unwind the beliefs that have become habits for many years. While they are destructive now, they might have been helpful at some point in the distant past and we do not want to be punitive with ourselves as we work towards these changes.

These beliefs are like deeply ingrained psychological dirt that we can gently wash away over time and with our repeated attention. Our approach to modifying our beliefs must be consistent, thoughtful and gentle.

Chapter 11: Using Gratitude and Forgiveness to Improve Our Relationships

In previous chapters, we used our intellect and willpower to enforce changes in our responses to life including our anger, guilt, fear and various beliefs. We can also create a better working environment and experience more richness by increasing our use of various virtues.

Gratitude

Gratitude is important because it creates a strong sense of support; we see life and those around us as contributing to our success and well-being. With gratitude as part of our mental makeup, we can dispel the gloom of anger, fear, and guilt. These dark moods cannot thrive in a world full of abundance.

Gratitude is not an object we can touch or hold in our hands. Instead, gratitude is an energy, an attitude, a motive, and a dynamic way of viewing all of life. Gratitude has the qualities of appreciation, thankfulness, respect, and generosity. This reminds me of a near-perfect description of the *opposite* of gratitude, as embodied by Charles Dickens' famous character Scrooge. At the beginning of the story, Scrooge is a "squeezing, wrenching, grasping, clutching, covetous old sinner." As most of us recall from the "The Christmas Carol", gratitude was a major healing antidote for Scrooge's psychological ailments.

To experience gratitude, we must make it a priority and add it to our work each day. For example, we can note that our work colleagues are critical components of the business and our success. They contribute in different ways with various levels of skills and talents, but also with their kindness, thoughtfulness, and interest in those they serve and work with. We can learn to observe their contributions, and whenever possible to give heartfelt thanks for what they do. *When was the last time you acknowledged gratitude to your staff, managers or fellow employees?*

Gratitude is more than a simple, "Thank you." True gratitude recognizes teamwork, collaboration, and that we all have various gifts. A great way to build this virtue is to spend a few minutes each day recalling examples of support in the office. As we become more aware of gratitude, we experience its fullness and how it brings us closer together. *Do you notice that you feel drawn closer to others when they express sincere gratitude?*

Some of us might find it difficult to see life or work as generous, and feel unable to express gratitude as a daily experience. One reason is that our criterion for observing generosity or expressing gratitude has too high of a threshold. In order for us to think gratefully, we need a promotion, have our boss praise us endlessly, be shown unending respect, or close a major new account. Big things have to happen for us to be grateful.

We might feel that the more mundane parts of work-life, when small things run smoothly, are too trite to be grateful for because this is the way things are "supposed" to be. We cannot imagine life supporting us unless events are out-of-the-ordinary, sudden, or dramatic. We are sometimes guilty of the same issue in other parts of our non-work lives, too, where we assume the kindness of our family, a comfortable home, and good health are entitlements we deserve and thus do not require our gratitude.

We can become blind to our good fortune because our minds resist the idea of feeling grateful for the small gifts in life. We need to open our eyes to the many small gifts that are far more common than large ones. The examples of support in life are too numerous to mention but they might include these small gratitudes:

- enjoying good health today
- having a good working mind
- being part of a meaningful project
- being helped by others
- a thoughtful boss
- a kind colleague
- a regular paycheck
- good training
- promotional opportunities
- the opportunity to learn new things

Can you recognize the many parts of your life that work well, versus the parts that perhaps need some improvement? Embracing life's small gifts with a grateful attitude creates a better work environment.

Over months and years of regular practice and attention, generosity and gratitude will come alive in all parts of our lives. *As we connect with this ever-present support and nourishment, our mental state shifts from, "Life is a struggle" to "I feel supported."*

When we are in a negative mood, or when we feel a loss of control and a sense that life is difficult and challenging, it is crucial to shift our perspective and see the world in a generous light. *Expressing gratitude produces a deeply nourishing energy that comforts us and gets us through those tough days.*

Personally, when I first started with this work, it was awkward and I felt a little silly. Much of what I did was to offer a pleasant platitude of "good job" or a simple "thank you" to my coworkers. With time, my mind has more readily accepted the truth that life is benevolent, and my experience of gratitude has developed into a more continual awareness of the generous and giving nature of life. Gratitude has also helped reduce my pessimism, fear, guilt and anger. As a result, I am more optimistic over-all. Gratitude has enabled me to be more stable in my mood and grounded in my expectations.

Building gratitude into our character requires a full commitment. It is not enough to work with gratitude only when business is booming, when it is convenient, or when we "feel good." This work must transcend any moods or whims. To build a virtue like gratitude requires effort similar to exercising to build up our physical body. We cannot build muscles without regular exercise and effort; nor can we build gratitude without looking for examples of generosity in our life and acknowledging them every day! We are establishing a relationship with gratitude. Like any relationship, it requires attention or it will wither and eventually cease to exist.

Working with gratitude does not always generate immediate results and we may not wake up one day full of unending gratitude as we see the full generosity of life. We are planting a seed that takes patience and care to germinate and grow.

While we can observe the world's generosity and the generosity of others, there are also difficulties to deal with. Imperfection abounds around us: cranky people, ill health, less-than-ideal relationships, our own immaturity, and bothersome technical issues at work. These issues will continue to pop up and require us to exercise smarter ways to manage them.

However, we can also observe the parts of our life that work well. This is analogous to working in a rose garden. There are always some weeds in the garden or thorns on the bushes (bad situations) but our primary attention is growing the roses (blessings or good things in our lives) that we wish to further experience. As gratitude blooms in our lives, it improves our sense of well-being.

Forgiveness

Forgiveness is another virtue that can be helpful in

the workplace, although some find it a challenge to embrace. There is the time-worn image of the offending person standing mournfully in front of the victim, asking for forgiveness, and the victim magnanimously accepting the apology while releasing the offending person from their transgressions. It looks too simple.

In addition we are subjected to public displays on TV or the Internet of a lofty individual caught in deceit, such as a transgression or corruption. The offender professes to take full responsibility for their actions, while gnashing their teeth and wailing their emotions. Some of these displays may be sincere and heartfelt, but others seem questionable and manipulative.

In today's society, we also have litigation as a suitable method of handling fault that bypasses the need for forgiveness. We extract a pound of flesh to create a sense that all is right in the world and we have been treated fairly and justly.

However, in all of the above situations, is this what we truly want? Do we experience a healing that leaves us with peace in our mind and body?

Forgiveness must be a great quality "par excellence" as it has been noted by philosophers, statesmen and key religious figures for centuries. Thus, there must be some practical ways to perceive and use forgiveness.

As a starting point, we need to understand the difference between forgiving and forgetting. We can choose to forgive, but will not likely forget. In fact, remembering an event is an excellent tool for learning. Our memories of previous events allow us to review various situations and find better ways to manage them in the future. For example, we can recall our subpar performance on a project, understand what we learned from the experience, and know what we need to do next time to achieve a better result.

Forgiveness is our active decision to stop directing our anger or irritation towards others, and it continues as we try to make amends and heal our wounds. It motivates us to find better methods of self-control. Forgiveness does not mean we have to befriend those who have violated us, but it does mean that we choose not to direct our own angry energies towards them and have made peace within ourselves.

Forgiveness must include our sincere attempt to make amends for our offensive actions. Making amends might be through physical, monetary, or verbal means. We must also take stock of our errors, acknowledge them, and create better skills and habits to make sure they do not happen again. This might include managing our own impatience, jealousy, anger, pettiness or unreasonable expectations.

We need to establish the criteria of what is worthy of an act of forgiveness. We cannot have one criterion for those situations when we have violated others and another for when we feel violated. The criteria must also remain constant when we look at scenarios involving a family member versus strangers, big businesses or government. An inconsistent criterion demeans the whole idea of forgiveness.

Is it reasonable that a colleague at work, a fellow driver on the freeway, or someone helping us in the store is deserving of the same respect and forgiveness as those closer to us? Should we not do everything possible to make amends and then stride to be a better person to all? Or shall we show favoritism and forgive others by an inconsistent standard? While this is a tough concept to live up to, setting the same standards for everyone gives meaning to working with forgiveness. Otherwise, it is nothing but an empty platitude.

Another step in cultivating forgiveness is to review our expectations of the other party involved in the issue. The other party could be a person, a company, the government or even us. We need to ask ourselves:

- Will others readily forgive us for our transgressions and be lenient when we apologize?
- When others are at fault, will they feel deeply sorry? Will they want to apologize to us while making amends and developing better self-control?

Of course, we have no idea if others will readily forgive us as they might have no interest in our apology or efforts to make amends. Instead they may remain angry and irritated and just want to extract their pound of flesh. Have you sometimes had no interest in forgiving others when you felt slighted? *The lesson learned here is the act of forgiveness is something we do ourselves regardless of what others choose to do.*

Forgiving others also has nothing to do with cancelling a call for justice or ceasing to ask others to take responsibility for their own actions. Forgiveness is not our judgment on the behavior or event; rather, it is our decision not to pursue anger, resentment, irritation or hate in response. *It is important to remember that "bringing others to justice" is not usually within our control, and we frequently do not have the skills, authority or insights to do so.*

We also have to watch out for a tendency to direct our anger and irritation towards others who violated us. We hope our anger will force them to be regretful and punish them for their errors. Directing anger towards others is a seductive belief that is actually a boomerang, increasing our own anger, irritation, and resentment. Our anger towards others does little to change them and does not hold them responsible for their actions—but it certainly fuels pain in our own minds and bodies. In fact, it can lower the chance for any possible resolution of the conflict, since many people respond to anger with avoidance or anger of their own.

We need to work with forgiveness in several difference scenarios. The goal in working with forgiveness is to reduce our irritation while improving our character and overall well-being. The following are several practical examples of working with forgiveness.

Forgiving Others

In this first hypothetical situation, we have contributed greatly to a major project in our company with our own ideas, hard work and creativity. While our supervisor expresses some appreciation for our work, we hear later that he is receiving significant accolades and all of the credit from senior management, while our name is never mentioned. We might feel hurt, angry, bitter, or violated. We might find ourselves lashing out at our supervisor behind his back or constantly obsessing in our mind about how unfair he is for taking credit for our own work.

So what do we do? How can we best manage this situation? While it is completely normal to initially respond with negative emotions, we need to turn them off as soon as possible. They are not going to solve anything and the only person who is going to feel worse by expressing them is us. Even if we tell our supervisor how we really feel, we are not guaranteed a satisfactory resolution—and in fact he may respond to our anger in a defensive way, making things even worse.

Our best approach is to take some time to calm down and realize that directed anger and irritation are bad for us. Instead, we can take stock of the situation, approach our manager and share our thoughts on feeling slighted and unrecognized. We are then in a position to have an adult conversation on the issue. It might be that he was not aware we felt slighted and he might not have experienced major kudos from his manager, even though we thought he did. He may become our advocate and work to get us the credit we deserve as a valued employee.

On the other hand, he might think we did not contribute that much to this project and we have overestimated our own contributions. And in fact, he might be right and we need to ponder further if we have an overinflated sense of our work and what we contribute. Or, he might decide that he wants the credit even though he knows we did most of the work. He might be a very insecure, self-serving boss and perhaps we need to look elsewhere for a better manager.

However, we need to realize that no matter what action we take, the use of our anger, bitterness or hurt over any period of time does not help resolve anything; we lose when we become overwhelmed with our negative emotions. If in fact others did slight us, our act of forgiveness and choosing not to be angry and bitter is not condoning their actions. Instead we are releasing ourselves from our own negative feelings and are working on healthier options to handle workplace conflict.

Being Forgiven

In the next hypothetical scenario, we are not the victim of bad people or a bad situation—we are the victimizer. We agreed to help a fellow colleague on an important project, but failed to do our part. Instead we put in the minimum time, effort, and creative thought, yet ended up sharing the benefits of the results. In essence, we have sown little and yet reaped the positive results while our colleague did most of the work. Has this ever happened to you? Let's put ourselves in our colleague's shoes for a moment. Most people experience a deep sense of irritation, anger or frustration in this scenario, and it is easy to understand why.

How do we handle this kind of situation?

We can first ask ourselves if the expectations of the project were clearly laid out. Did both parties agree on the workload, determine it was fair and then do their part? There also needs to be some assurances that both parties are well-trained and competent in their respective roles. Otherwise, one party will be forced to do more work just to make up for the deficiencies of the less-trained or skilled individual.

Let's assume the workload was laid out correctly, but we did not do our part and now our colleague has confronted us with the issue. What do we do? We need to listen carefully to their complaints, avoid being defensive, and determine how to avoid this issue in the future. We need to take responsibility and accept the errors of our actions. We can ask ourselves if the problem is due to our own laziness, taking advantage of others, or simply an oversight on our part where we thought we were doing enough but did not meet the other party's expectations.

We can also try to make amends by offering to do a share of their work in the future. We are hopeful that the other offended party will accept our apologies and maintain a good working relationship. *However, there are no guarantees they will and we can only do our best in the future while making amends in the present.*

There is one other special circumstance that comes into play in this scenario and that is working with a controlling person who inherently does not trust others. They think if they do not do it, nobody will do it right and thus they take on too much work, exhaust themselves and then become angry. In this situation, we have to stand up for ourselves and demand our fair share of the work. Controlling people are a serious pathology in the workplace because they send the message that nobody is as good or as trainable as they are.

Self-forgiveness

Working to correct any areas where we have made mistakes or wronged others raises the question: should we forgive ourselves? Some might think we should not forgive ourselves for our own mistakes because we are flawed human beings and will always make blunders. Others think self-forgiveness creates narcissistic and self-absorbed people with no concern for others, who are unable to learn from past mistakes.

However, self-forgiveness is essential for healing. Our life has been full of mistakes and we will make more in the future. Remembering our mistakes is invaluable so we can learn to avoid them by developing various new talents. However, our own self-condemnation alone will not make us a better person. We become a better person by recognizing our errors, making amends, finding better ways to handle the situation differently in the future, and building new skills. This is lot more than simply saying, "I am sorry" and asking for forgiveness.

In addition, constant criticism beyond remembering a simple mistake causes massive mental irritation and self-loathing. If we readily forgive others and never forgive ourselves, aren't we telling ourselves everyone else is better than us and we alone are undeserving of forgiveness? It leaves us stuck in an endless cycle of unworthiness that makes us less able to help ourselves or anyone else. How can we be of help to others if we believe we are chronically incompetent?

We must see mistakes as stepping-stones to becoming a better person.

In dealing with common human problems, the root cause of many people's problems is a deep feeling of self-rejection and self-denial. They feel that because they make mistakes, they have little to offer and are worthless. We can ascertain if this is the case with us as we ask ourselves the following questions:

- Do we have difficulty readily accepting the praise of others?
- Are we hesitant about new opportunities?
- Do we frequently worry we will fail?
- Are we obsessed with loss and do we ruminate on our past losses?
- Are we afraid to admit our mistakes?

There is a tremendous benefit to viewing our own mistakes with compassion and accepting that others make mistakes, too. By acknowledging our own transgressions and making amends, we become more understanding of others. We are all a work-in-progress and as we recognize this in others and ourselves, we become more empathetic and understanding. This makes it easier to forgive others, because we see parts of our own immature self in them.

Final Thoughts

Most of our internalized anger and fear are born out of many small, poorly managed issues. Over time and without the use of forgiveness, these issues and baggage accumulate and fill us with excessive anger. This anger slowly consumes us and overshadows the rest of our humanity. *If unchecked, we can become a walking bundle of resentment, bitterness and anger as we lose our joy, peacefulness and enthusiasm for living.*

We need to learn to "give up" our right to apologies for recent or long-past injuries, wounds, and losses. We have to stop keeping score. It is not uncommon for people to make too much of old wounds and injuries versus what they have become in spite of various challenges in life. And we all have challenges! We need to see the value of no longer demanding reparations, holding onto our anger and creating misery within ourselves. With every trip we take down our memory lane of old hurts—from recent times, or from years or decades ago when we have chosen not to forgive—we reopen these painful wounds and relive the misery again.

There are people who are challenging and difficult to be around and work with. They carry a constant chip on their shoulder, are obnoxious, derogatory, and insulting. This is part of living; we all have to deal with these types of people. If we look closely, these people have their own issues and demons and are likely doing their best but may be unaware or insensitive to the damage they cause. They cannot see the results of their actions. Through our work with forgiveness, we can learn to be more understanding of these personalities as we see part of us in them. This does not condone the bad behavior of others and we should not become another person's doormat. But, forgiveness allows us to withhold our anger, be more understanding that others have issues too, and then find a better way to work with these people.

Being permanently angry might help some people validate that they have a legitimate gripe for their apparent victimization and oppressive life, but this is a massive price to pay in terms of mental irritation, bitterness, and self-pity. Long-term negative emotional reactions to difficult events do not promote healing; instead, this way of being only prolongs our pain.

The deeper value of working with forgiveness is that it connects us with our own humanity. Forgiveness makes us aware that we are one of many striving for self-improvement, better character, and amends for past mistakes. We are working alongside others to find new ways to accentuate healthy qualities such as peace, joy, gratitude, and kindness while reducing our anger, fear, sadness and guilt.

As people collectively embrace forgiveness, they are more inclined to reach out and help others. This is a fundamental principle of forgiveness: we all make mistakes and need help while we collectively strive to improve our character and humanity.

Chapter 12: Building Patience and Tolerance

Patience

Many of us view patience as waiting, enduring and suffering passively without complaint. *Companies may view patience as indecision, a lack of urgency, or weakness on the part of leadership.* Have you ever attended a sales or production meeting where patience was strongly encouraged? Instead, the focus is typically on how to get this done *now*.

However, we can discover many examples of impatience resulting in significant short- or long-term problems. These include:

- We fail to manage an inherently slow process (like R&D or Regulatory Affairs) and make things worse by obsessing about it or pushing too hard.

- We succumb to our emotional whims of urgency without evaluating the potential impacts our actions can have.
- Our impatience can give rise to physical discomfort like headaches, backaches or illness due to our failure to achieve a pace of activity that is impossible.
- We can impatiently push our subordinates too hard, versus respecting them for their achievements and contributions.
- Our perfectionist tendency to reach a goal by next week or the next day sets us up to fail.
- We miss a promotion at work, become upset, and fail to realize that we are progressing and learning new skills. We cannot see the time is not yet right for our next step.
- We become fearful that if we do not act quickly in response to an issue, disaster will result or an opportunity will disappear. Our despair can lead to poor decisions based upon fear rather than a well-thought-out process.
- We fail to focus on our long-term goals.

We need to see patience in a new light: not as something to avoid or frown upon, but instead as a virtue leading to better results. *Patience allows us to see the great potential for growth as we work through delays.*

Patience is a creative and dynamic energy that gives

us the capacity to understand a current situation and take advantage of any future opportunities. It helps us discern the best action and the best time to act. *It is our readiness to act quickly tempered by our commitment to do so in the ideal time.* Patience involves creating a goal, formulating a plan and then executing our plan at the right time.

Without patience, it is easy to assume we have failed in something, versus knowing we have just taken another step in the process of development. Patience educates us that our thoughts of failure are sometimes premature because the process is not yet finished. With patience, we acknowledge that it takes time to develop skills, character and intelligent decision-making, because life is complex.

Patience is the intelligent control of how we pace ourselves, understand our limits and the limits of other people, and the laws and forces we must live with and adhere to. Patience allows for our perceptive use of resources in a timely manner.

We must also be wary of confusing patience with laziness and apathy. We do not want to just "go with the flow" but instead we should be fully prepared to act dynamically when the time is right.

Developing patience allows us to:

- Act wisely with a well-thought-out and detailed plan.
- Maximize our efforts by acting at the right time.
- Realize that doing nothing is sometimes the best choice.
- Recognize that it might be our stubbornness, inflexibility, critical nature or lack of self-control that is the cause of our delays.
- Acknowledge that better preparation is necessary or a better opportunity is yet to come.
- Understand the larger patterns, purposes and principles behind our decisions.
- Exercise strong self-control to subdue our immature reactions to delays.
- Understand what we can control versus what we cannot control.
- Realize that life has rhythms, just like the seasons. There is a time for planting and a time for harvesting. Patience teaches us that we usually cannot sow and reap on the same day.
- Promote healthy collaboration when we work together with others and gather valued input towards making the best decisions.
- Realize the process of progress can only go so fast. We do not have full control of all of the factors and people in our environment that

influence the pace of a project. We learn about our limits.

- Push back on excessive activity: our tendency to confuse activity with achievement versus taking intelligent action.
- Ask the questions: "Why am I doing this and what is the benefit? Will it be helpful to all or create problems? What are all the ramifications of this decision?"

Patience is not a static process, but a dynamic and valuable part of our character. We need to see its value while embracing what we learn during the times we cannot see actual progress. Instead, we must recognize that our strong efforts are playing out under the surface of our awareness. They are creating new "roots" of a strong foundation for our future success. It is like a wound healing from surgery. It takes time to see obvious results, although the process of healing starts immediately.

Tolerance

Tolerance suggests a just, objective, and non-judgmental attitude toward others whose opinions, practices, race, religion, nationality, or gender is different from ours. The need for tolerance is evident as we work to overcome our criticism of others relating to the way they act or how we perceive their skills. In a broader scope, the lack of tolerance is our response to something that we perceive as wrong, harmful or different. It can result in reactions of disgust, bitterness, vengeance or resentment.

So how does this apply to the workplace and what can we do about it? This section will include examples of intolerance in the workplace; primarily the subtle ways we are intolerant outside of the commonly discussed issues of race, gender, nationality or religion. We will then review various approaches to creating tolerance that will further improve our workplace environment and personal sense of well-being.

The first point is to establish if we might have an issue with intolerance of others and ourselves. The following are some questions to ponder:

- Do we sometimes lash out at, or feel threatened by, authority, our colleagues or our competition? (Our competition could be both within our company or in another company.) How often is this part of our conversations and thoughts throughout the day?
- Is our anger, resentment or bitterness because they have harmed us directly though overt actions, or is it because they are different then us?

- Do we resent our boss even though he/she is generally a good manager? Do we not like taking direction from others because we think we already know it all?
- Do we get upset at our colleagues because they do things differently than we would, and we think their methods are either stupid, inferior or threatening?
- In addition, do we see our competition or other companies as an "evil" that is out to destroy our livelihood and us? Are we afraid that there is not enough opportunity to go around and thus we must wipe out our competitors?
- Is our intolerance a function of our own lack of success? Do we find ourselves jealous of others? Do we rejoice in seeing others fail, rather than encouraging and congratulating them on their achievements while working to improve ourselves?
- Do we find ourselves intolerant of others as they fail to live up to a desired level of performance? Do we berate others and put them down? Is it possible they may be living up to their full potential in a given role and they are doing their best? Are our standards too high, or perhaps others need more training or to be reassigned to another role that is a better fit?
- Are we intolerant of ourselves when we fail? Are we always on the hunt for a scapegoat or

someone else to blame? Can it ever be that we either made a mistake or did not have the skills to manage a project? Are we unable to admit to ourselves when we have failed and instead become overwhelmed with humiliation or anger and incapable of learning from the experience?

- Do we ever tell ourselves that everything would work out just fine if we did not have to deal with people? Do we constantly think other people create and are the cause of our problems? Have we gone from job to job because "other people" have frequently created dismay for us? Have we ever considered that we might be a part of the problem too?

- Do we continually think others mistreat us? Does this idea extend to every company we have worked for, to every relationship or to every difficulty we have had to manage?

- Are we someone who is habitually critical, argumentative and fault-finding? Do we get a thrill from being intolerant as we look for the weaknesses in others and attack them? Have we ever considered that this habit may be our own attempt to be controlling or feel better about ourselves? Is it possible we need to work on our own self-esteem?

- Do certain types of people really bother us and push our buttons? Could these people be pushy, aggressive, self-centered or defensive?

Maybe what we dislike so much in others is also what we dislike in ourselves?

- Do we find fault mainly as the way to boost our ego—as if everything we do has to be the standard of greatness and excellence in the world?

- Do we gossip? Is our subject matter usually others and their deficiencies? Do we lack the courage or compassion to confront or help others directly versus talking behind their backs? Moreover, does our gossip help us feel better about our own shortcomings?

- Are we cliquish? Do we belong to some type of "good old boy" network that is isolated from others? Do we see ourselves as superior and apart from many other people in the company? Have we considered we need to work together collectively and garner the input of others in order to achieve the best results?

- Intolerance grows as we put our attention and focus on it. Do you ever notice that when the media discusses intolerance and rails on it repeatedly with no apparent solutions, the problem becomes magnified and more inflamed by all parties?

Having identified some areas of intolerance in our own character, what can we do about it? How can we build tolerance in ourselves?

We create tolerance largely by eliminating our ignorance and negative responses to something we believe is different, wrong or harmful. We need to see differences not in a negative light but as a normal part of the diversity of life. Simple observation shows the massive diversity of plants, minerals, animals and people. We live in a very heterogeneous world that gives rise to balance and interdependence. Consider the food chain within the entire planet and the great level of interdependence that each species has on one another. The same applies to plant life with various ecosystems that attract the necessary moisture, sunlight, animal life and soil nutrients that is necessary for prosperity.

In the same way, our work environment consists of many varieties of people. Some are smarter than others, work better with their hands, have superior strategic skills, are well-equipped to manage repetitive or detailed work, or are excellent with numbers. In fact, each employee brings a unique skill-set and personality that when placed appropriately can serve to better the functioning of the whole.

We are not all the same. Treating others with respect and thoughtfulness does not mean expecting everyone to behave the same, think the same, or have identical skills and potential. The same is true with our bodies; every part of us from our ears to our nose, our fingers to our legs, plays an important and useful role. Thus, our differences are not an excuse to be upset, but instead are a necessary part of our company's health. *At the same time, we need to recognize the importance that everyone plays in creating our company's balanced and diversified environment.* We need to realize that the diversity of a group of people can bring forth more ideas and better creativity to help us collectively prosper.

The other area we can ponder is our anger or frustration for what we see as wrong or harmful from the behavior and actions of others. There are rare cases when an individual or group is clearly behaving badly to the detriment of others in the workplace. This cannot continue and action is required to remedy the problem.

More commonly, we will observe people of good character behaving badly or not measuring up to their full potential. Maybe it is because they had a bad day at home, feel ill, or are frustrated because they are over their head or their boss chewed them out. Whatever the reason, this happens at some point with most people. We can respond to their anger, irritation or snippiness with the same behavior ourselves—or we can exhibit tolerance and understanding. *We do not have to condone their behavior, but we can express compassion.* It is not necessary to respond to bad behavior with more hatred or bitterness. Instead of collecting and harboring our sense of injustice, discrimination and anger, we can collect joy, affection and gratitude.

It is very easy to find fault. Everywhere we look, we can find the need for improvement, including in ourselves. What takes work, imagination, and goodwill is finding and acknowledging things to praise. Yes, there are many things that we can legitimately criticize, but there are also many things worthy of praise. We fail to praise when our default response to life is negativity.

Tolerance requires a generous and charitable heart that is willing to overlook minor imperfections in order to embrace actual and potential good aspects. In addition, even when we note significant faults in others, our basic goodwill and vision can enable us to act and speak constructively about these issues instead of attacking others with criticism and condemnation. If there are genuine faults and mistakes, the solution is trying to figure out what we can say or do to help—or at least begin the process of turning things around.

There are times when we must learn to practice detachment. This is our attempt to stop taking everything personally and instead become a witness to what is going on around us. In essence, we stop jumping into every bit of nastiness or crabbiness shown by others. If we are confident that our colleagues are good people of character, we know their bursts of immaturity will pass. *We can focus on the ideal of who they are and what they are trying to become, rather than their occasional outbursts.*

We must not confuse tolerance with indifference or full acceptance. There is a large class of behaviors that may not be up to par and deserve neither harsh criticism nor approval. Instead, they need more work and effort. We must focus on the potential for improvement, much like observing a young child learning the piano and understanding that mistakes are a necessary part of learning. In general, those who think in black-and-white terms (without shades of gray) find it difficult to cultivate this appropriate attitude. *They cannot see when something is imperfect but moving in the right direction.*

The environment in which tolerance thrives (and is sustained) is one in which we have a basic cheerful attitude about life and are comfortable in who we are. On the other hand, people who are perpetually unhappy and dissatisfied—if not outright bitter—tend to find fault far too often. Their intolerance is the child of their personal discontent. Intolerance is often a minor symptom of a much larger problem of depression, self-criticism and lack of fulfillment or joy in living.

We can also cultivate the habit of focusing on what is right in the world, right with other people, and right about ourselves. We can remain focused on our principles, our values, our high standards of relating to others, and our efforts to work harder on who we want to become.

To cultivate tolerance we must extend goodwill to all groups, regardless of their behavior. Even when the person has not registered their mistake or repented, we must be tolerant, recognizing that our own anger and frustration only makes things worse. *Sometimes those who make mistakes are blind versus acting intentionally cruel or thoughtlessly. Our most important activity should be praise and focusing on the ideal versus on what is wrong. The key to tolerance is to see all that is right with life. What percentage of the time do we spend focused on what is wrong versus what is right in our life?*

In the end, tolerance acknowledges that there is a rich variety of difference in the human race—in talent, experience, and competence—and yet all blend together for the betterment of everyone. While there is imperfection, we can view the best in each of us by nurturing and praising what is beneficial.

Chapter 13: Finding Meaning in Our Work

Meaning, as I am defining it here, is an appreciation and gratefulness that our efforts, struggles, accomplishments, and commitments have value. This is highly motivating and can serve as a great platform with which to build a career. While it would be easier if there were a concrete list of steps we could check off to create meaning, meaning is not generally born this way. Our journey to meaning involves setbacks and partial successes as we struggle to achieve our goals, uphold our values and overcome difficulties along the way.

We build significant meaning from:

- overcoming difficulties and challenges.
- our continual commitment to express higher ideals or virtues.
- subordinating our immature whims and desires.

We can motivate ourselves with personal comfort, mental or emotional excitement, or material goods and avoid anything that causes us discomfort or stress. But is this the best way to approach our work and our lives? Building meaning changes this paradigm by helping us see the value of difficulties, rather than viewing them as disasters and seeing ourselves as victims. Meaning helps us establish boundaries and understand our role in the interconnected world. It allows us to wrap our mind around events in life, give them perspective and relate to similar situations in the past, present and future. We can take satisfaction in knowing our difficult accomplishments create wisdom, contributing to our character and the person we are today.

Those who actively search for meaning and value in who they are, what they do, and how they respond are far more able to learn from their experiences than those who just drift through life doing only what is required and merely reacting to events—often with anger, discouragement, or anxiety.

As our understanding grows about the value of our difficulties, we move through our daily tasks with less friction, more acceptance, and eventually more joy in performing work that is well done. Many employees struggle with annoyance about the drudgery, demeaning or disgusting aspects of their work. Yet we all know that every job has these issues. As we learn the significance of our work, including the value of even the boring and routine aspects, it removes much of the lingering annoyance about having to bear less-than-ideal experiences.

Meaning Through Overcoming Problems

It is common to experience frustration or disappointment as we work through challenges. Many people respond with the well-worn method of anger, fear or guilt. While these emotional responses can initially motivate us to take action and look for solutions, if we allow them to continue, they can bog us down and send us to the misery pit of despair and self-pity. As a result, we see our hard-fought efforts more as a wound in our consciousness versus a challenge we have learned to overcome. This can leave us feeling bitter instead of inspired.

By focusing on our wounds, we recreate the pain each time we visit the memory. Little damage remains in us other than the damage we continue to put on ourselves by reliving the old disappointing memories and giving them energy and power over us. From time to time, we need to cultivate an insightful frame of mind and review—not relive— some of our painful experiences.

We need to view our problems in a new light: not as a curse, but as a chance to learn and develop. Our mental, emotional and physical discomfort serve as great educators. We either can get upset by the presence of problems, or see them as an opportunity to use our best creative skills. Think of approaching a crossword puzzle, when we are engrossed in finding the right answers. Why not approach all of life's problems in this manner? Yes, life will inevitably confront us with problems and difficulties: nobody is immune. Our history and experiences in the past are fixed, but we can change our interpretations of these past events.

Life's difficulties and challenges are the foundation of acquiring knowledge. Our experiences of learning to drive a car, play the piano, study for a test, achieve good grades, develop friendships, or parent children all have challenges. Living a life free of problems is not only impossible, but would mean living a life without growth. Our development occurs gradually as we overcome our problems. Through difficulties, we can learn:

- wisdom from solving problems
- courage from overcoming danger
- trust from our previous successes

- patience and persistence from being forced to wait
- compassion from our own struggles
- adaptability and creativity from trying new ideas
- gratitude from our previous losses
- how to make changes and stop repeating the same mistakes
- how much better and wiser we are because of our life challenges
- what to let go of because it is not serving us
- what is really important

We can also use curiosity to inspire creativity in solving our problems. Instead of becoming overwhelmed with anger, fear or guilt, we can invoke our creativity by asking ourselves questions such as:

- What is the real issue here? Have I carefully identified the problem?
- Is the problem due to my lack of skills or knowledge and, if so, how can I learn what is needed?
- Am I getting in my own way? Are some of my own biases or distorted beliefs adding to the problem?
- Have I reached out to others for help and assistance, or am I embarrassed that I cannot find my own solutions?

- Do I lack several qualities of character that are contributing to the problem such as a lack of patience, resilience, responsibility or adaptability?
- Are my expectations of performance unrealistic and I am setting myself up for continual failure?
- Have I failed to trust others and taken on an unrealistic burden?

As we work with curiosity, it is important that we look honestly at the answers to our questions. This honest appraisal is difficult for many people. Most of us naturally fight any thought that we have failed. We need to recognize that challenges, dilemmas and our own mistakes are opportunities for growth rather than statements that we are "stupid" or "a failure."

There might be times when a perfect result is not possible. We cannot always create a win-win for everyone, including ourselves. We can see this as either a glass half-full or a glass half-empty. We need to keep our focus on the glass as half-full. This is the right choice for creating optimism and enthusiasm versus pessimism and gloom as we work through problems.

Dealing With Significant Challenges

You might wonder how we find meaning in significant challenges like the loss of a job, recovering from serious mistakes or contracting a major illness. Certain problems are extremely uncomfortable and create great hardship. The long-term value is not easily apparent, but we can still learn and gain from the experience.

We can learn:

- to immediately sort out and give attention to what is most important; that is, set clear boundaries, limit attention and responsibility, focus on what is urgent and important right now, and keep it this way. When there is too much to do, little time, and little energy, we must learn to discern and focus on the truly important items and largely ignore the rest.
- to recognize what we cannot control and cannot do and just accept it. Good boundaries keep us from wasting our energy on what we cannot change or influence. This includes cutting off our tendency for self-pity, panic, and anger.
- to become introverted and highly aware of our inner and outer resources. We can mobilize them, protect them, and apply them with great efficiency.

- to discover who our friends are (and are not) in times of crisis and how many are willing to provide comfort and support.
- how strong and resourceful we are—especially our capacity for self-control, endurance, and managing our emotional reactions of fear, anger, disgust, or discouragement. Unless we just give up, we will come out of these episodes more centered in our strength, confident about any future challenges, and proud of how well we are able to manage life's obstacles.

Meaning Through Building Virtues or Ideals

Some people experience a significant amount of meaning as they focus their activities and thought processes around various noble ideals, values or virtues.

Regardless of what we are doing or where we are, we often express our strong beliefs through our actions. I wrote about the concept of ideals or virtues in Chapter Two as part of a self-evaluation exercise. These virtues or ideals are abstract; they are not things we can touch. They are numerous and include, among others: joyfulness, humility, wisdom, generosity, patience, kindness, faithfulness, thoughtfulness, self-control, love, charity, responsibility, courage, discipline, integrity, respect, and perseverance.

To help create a profound level of meaningfulness in our work-life, we can develop and focus our attention on upholding various noble virtues in our speech, actions, attitudes, and thoughts. So where does this lead us? The following are some of the implications of working with virtues or ideals to create a meaningful life:

We make better decisions. How often have you sat through meetings and been confronted with multiple options to consider? As we sift through all of the options and their implications, we usually target such things as product quality, a more efficient process, meeting the demands of the customer, or upholding our obligations to our stockholders. We do this in a thoughtful manner and take into account the impact our decisions have on all of the involved parties.

However, we can also add the use of virtues or values to our decision process. For example, we can focus our attention on the highest qualities of integrity and respect and decide if our decision upholds these principles. In another example, we might have a conflict with a colleague and ask ourselves, "How can I use self-control, patience or kindness in this situation?" On the other hand, we can be struggling within ourselves and frustrated with our lack of progress on a certain project. As we pursue new approaches to solving this problem, we can focus on our best qualities of perseverance, courage and self-control. All of these qualities compliment the decision process and result in a better outcome.

We build stronger relationships. If we review the previous list of virtues, it is easy to recognize that anyone practicing and living these qualities daily would be very agreeable to work with. This is much more than just being a nice, friendly person. It is choosing to be of a certain character, and committing ourselves to the hard work to modify our behavior. The net effect is that our work relations can flourish.

We give our life more focus and strengthen our sense of identity. This expands our sense-of-self beyond events or accomplishments. Have you ever noticed the biographies of various people on Linked-in, in the newspaper or as they are introduced at meetings? They usually speak about their accomplishments and life progression. It is generally a data-dump of facts, and while the facts may be impressive and significant, they frequently tell us little about the whole person. Even when I interview candidates and ask them questions about their values and identity, I tend to receive answers about what they have done rather than who they are. They do not discuss their character and values.

Yet, most people relate to and identify with who a person *is* versus what they have done. Unfortunately, not everyone takes the time to decide what they stand for, the qualities they hold dear, and the values they live for. They may do some of this work subconsciously, but it is far more powerful when we do it consciously. By doing so, we create an identity and can act with decisiveness.

We gain strength to endure difficult times. Developing and living various virtues is difficult and this lifestyle is frequently in conflict with our desire for comfort. For example, our commitment to patience and understanding can be a challenge when we work with unreasonable and self-absorbed people. Alternatively, we might struggle to handle the moodiness of others or long hours at work. We gain strength as we learn to rise above the feeling that it is "too hard" or that others do not appreciate our sacrifice. We do this by prioritizing the virtues of commitment and teamwork.

Our bad moods and negative pressure from others have less influence on us. As we incorporate our values and virtues into our daily process, we build a strong identity—in other words, we know who we are. Yes, we listen to others and their input, but we will partially filter this input based upon our own values. We do not have to go along with the opinion of everyone else. We can also stop the automatic reactions of our subconscious that drives our outdated emotional responses of anger, fear or guilt. Instead, we more readily think for ourselves and stand firm in our convictions. We also become less subject to invalidators: those people who constantly demean our ideas or contributions based upon their own personal wants and desires. We can still listen to them, but we avoid getting caught up in their ability to negatively influence us.

We maintain our own high standards. We establish and live by a set of standards based upon our values. We are no longer subject to lowering our standards to "go with the flow" but instead we remain firm in our convictions.

We experience the virtue or value within ourselves. I was surprised to find this *side benefit* of working with values or virtues. As we use them, they not only guide our behavior and thinking process—

they also become our experience. For example, as we work to build gratitude, tolerance, forgiveness, or patience, we not only behave this way, but we experience these qualities within ourselves. Virtues add a new dimension of richness to our internal experiences.

We learn to flush away what is not important.
Over time, our process of including virtues and values in our thinking and actions result in a better realization of what we need to let go of. Our attention on the bad things in life, our disappointments and painful wounds, become easier to release. When confronted in the light of positive qualities like gratitude and joy, the darkness of anger, fear, resentment or humiliation are no longer valuable. In essence, these negative qualities are absorbed and overwhelmed by the positive qualities we build into our character.

It is important to remember that, like anything, virtues can be taken to the extreme. We can suffocate people with love. We can overwhelm people with our kindness, to the point where they do not learn self-sufficiency. Our zeal for patience can become complacency. We must always temper our use of any virtue with common sense. In excess, they can all be damaging and unbalanced.

The work of developing and experiencing meaning is not an automatic or easy process. Learning to see the value of our struggles, as well as committing to building noble virtues, requires sacrifice on our part. This includes giving up our old grievances, humiliations or self-pity as we process and find meaning in our struggles. We build virtues by committing to an ideal, denying our immature nature, rejecting our automatic responses of anger, fear and guilt and our desire to *just be comfortable.*

The payoff for our efforts is that we will stand firm in the noble qualities we value, perceive our struggles as worthwhile, and build our character. We know who we are and can contribute the fullness of ourselves in all we do.

193

194

ABOUT THE AUTHOR

James Patterson is a California native and received a Masters of Science degree in Biochemistry from Michigan State University. He spent 14 years working for a number of clinical diagnostic medical companies in research and development and sales. James has spent the last 23+ years as a medical recruiter working with medical businesses on a national level to identify and hire professionals in roles that include research and development, sales and marketing, regulatory affairs, operations, manufacturing, and senior management. Life has gifted James with two beautiful daughters, an amazing wife of 38+ years, many encouraging and outstanding friends, exceptional work colleagues, and good fortune in many areas of his life.

James Patterson

Make Your Career Meaningful: A Practical Toolbox

Made in the USA
San Bernardino, CA
01 December 2015